The Alchemy of Happiness

Sources and Studies in World History

The Alchemy of Happiness

Abû Ḥâmid Muḥammad al-Ghazzâlî

Translated by Claud Field

Revised and Annotated by Elton L. Daniel

M.E. Sharpe Inc.

Armonk, New York

London, England

Available in the United Kingdom and Europe from M. E. Sharpe, Publishers, 3 Henrietta Street, London WC2E 8LU.

Library of Congress Cataloging-in-Publication Data

Ghazzālī, 1058–1111.
[Kīmiyā–yi sa' ādat. English. Selections]
The alchemy of happiness / author Abu Hamid Muhammad al–Ghazzali ; translator Claud Field ; revised and annotated by Elton L. Daniel.
p. cm.—(Sources and studies in world history)
Translations of: Kīmiyā–yi sa' ādat.
Includes bibliographical references.
ISBN 1–56324–004–1 (hard).—ISBN 1–56324–005–X (pbk.)
1. Islamic ethics—Early works to 1800. I. Field, Claud, 1863–1941.
II. Title. III. Series.
B753.G33K413 1991
297'.5—dc20 91-9523
CIP

Printed in the United States of America

MV 10 9 8 7 6

To My Parents
and the Memory of My Grandparents

Contents

Foreword

This volume introduces a series called *Sources and Studies in World History*. The series attempts to satisfy a variety of needs in the emerging field of world history. It will publish titles in global, comparative, and regional history as well as works of methodological or pedagogical value to teachers and scholars of world history. The series will include primary sources as well as secondary interpretations, anthologies as well as complete works, and the results of new research as well as classic studies in the field. Its intended audience embraces all who desire to make sense of human history, from the college classroom to the world stage.

The Alchemy of Happiness answers a need for important primary sources in the study of world history. While the canon of sources for Western history receives daily attention, historians have only recently begun to identify, translate, edit, and make available the significant works of non-Western cultures. Perhaps nowhere is the paucity of accessible sources more of a problem than in the study of Islam. Long simmering animosities, profound cultural differences, and problems of translation have left much of Islamic literature, philosophy, and culture unknown to the American public and unavailable to students.

Elton Daniel shows us here what we have missed. In revising and annotating the Claud Field translation of *The Alchemy*, Daniel presents al-Ghazzâlî with a clarity and directness that almost makes us forget that the text was written nearly one thousand years ago. We hear the great Muslim philosopher as he must have been heard by his students in Baghdad in 1092; we read him at the height of his persuasive powers, as he was read by untold followers in numerous languages. And yet, we also are able to recognize the gulf that separates the sensibilities of the devout Sufi-influenced theologian from the secular scholarship of modern culture. As Daniel reminds us at the beginning of his preface, a reading of al-Ghazzâlî not only introduces us to the rich spiritual world of Islam, it also serves as one of many possible introductions to the world of intense religious feeling that we have lost.

Kevin Reilly

Preface

In studying the history of world civilizations, few if any concepts are more difficult for people of modern times to comprehend than the intense religiosity which characterized so many civilizations—medieval European, Byzantine, Islamic, Indian, East Asian—during the period from the fall of the classical empires to the beginning of the European expansion. Whether because of the pervasive secularity of modern civilization, or the blatant materialism of contemporary life, or simply because of the rigid compartmentalization of religious life (such as it is) well away from social and political existence, it is not easy to appreciate the spiritual sentiments that once impelled so many people to fight each other in the name of religion, to flock to monasteries or ascetic retreats, to pour their creative and artistic energies into religious works, or to govern every aspect of their lives with a piety founded on transcendent scriptural ideals.

One work which surely captures and vividly expresses the essence of the pre-modern religious spirit is *The Alchemy of Happiness*, written by perhaps the greatest and certainly one of the most original of Muslim thinkers, Abû Ḥâmid Muḥammad al-Ghazzâlî. In composing *The Alchemy of Happiness*, Ghazzâlî not only outlined a comprehensive world-view based on the religion of Islam, he also specifically attempted to demonstrate how all human behavior should be guided by a religious faith as intense and unshakably certain as it was all encompassing. It is precisely these two concepts—the extension of religious piety into all phases of life and the constant link between faith and action—which tend to be the most alien to contemporary, and particularly Western, culture. Thus, Ghazzâlî's treatise is of exceptional value to those seeking insights into this ancient and very different understanding of the world.

The Life and Works of Ghazzâlî

Abû Ḥâmid Muḥammad, son of Muḥammad, al-Ghazzâlî was born to a family of spinners and sellers of wool in a small village in the environs of the city of Ṭûs in eastern Iran in the year 450 after the hijra (1058 A.D.).[1] Ghazzâlî, or alternatively Ghazâlî, the descriptive name (called in Arabic the *nisba*) by which he is generally known, may be explained as either a reference to his occupation in the wool trade (*ghazzâla*) or to the name of his home village (Ghazâl). His father having vowed that his son should be dedicated to the service of Islam, Ghazzâlî received the education appropriate to becoming a Muslim scholar, first at a mosque school to learn the rudimentary skills and then at an institution known as a *madrasa*, which was emerging as the main center for advanced formal instruction in the theory and practice of Islamic law. On his own, Ghazzâlî also developed an early interest in Sufism, the Islamic form of individual and organized religious mysticism, and received private instruction in the ways of its practitioners, the Sufis. It was, however, his command of Muslim jurisprudence which first brought him fame; after studying in madrasas in his native Ṭûs and the city of Jurjân (modern Gorgân), he became a protégé of the famous

[1] Modern biographical studies of Ghazzâlî include Duncan Macdonald, "The Life of al-Ghazzâlî," *Journal of the American Oriental Society* 20(1899):71-132; W. Gardener, *An Account of al-Ghâzâlî's Life and Works* (Madras, 1919); S. M. Zwemer, *A Moslem Seeker after God* (London, 1920); Dwight Donaldson, "Mohammed al-Ghazzali," *Muslim World* 11(1921):377-88; Margaret Smith, *Al-Ghazâlî the Mystic* (London, 1944); and W. M. Watt, *Muslim Intellectual* (Edinburgh, 1963).

theologian and scholar of the Shâfi^{c}î school of Islamic law, the Imâm al-Ḥaramayn Abu'l-Ma^{c}âlî ^{c}Abd al-Malik al-Juvaynî, at the madrasa in Nishapur from 470/1077-78 down to the death of Juvaynî in 478/1085. In addition to continuing his interest in Sufism, Ghazzâlî also began to develop ideas not typical of the conventional legal scholar of his day, in particular his belief that such scholars should master a variety of academic fields of study, not just those necessary for law itself, and that guidance in problems of religious law should be based on something more than simply following the opinions of previous jurisconsults, a practice known as *taqlîd* or "imitation."

After Juvaynî's death, Ghazzâlî was sufficiently prominent to attract the attention of the powerful statesman Niẓâm al-Mulk and through his patronage to be admitted to the court of Malik Shâh, the Seljuk Turkish sultan who was the real political master of most of the eastern half of the Muslim world. This led, in 484/1091, to his appointment as a professor at the greatest institution of Sunni Muslim learning of the age, the Niẓâmiyya Madrasa in Baghdad. In this capacity, it was inevitable that Ghazzâlî would be caught up in the political affairs of the capital, and this may have led him into trouble after the assassination of his mentor Niẓâm al-Mulk in 485/1092 and the subsequent death of Malik Shâh. In the succession struggle between Barkyârûq and his uncle Tutush, Ghazzâlî probably favored Tutush. When Barkyârûq came to power in 488/1095 and put Tutush to death, Ghazzâlî's position would have thus become precarious.

In any event, it was in that very year that Ghazzâlî experienced what he describes in his famous autobiography, *The Deliverance from Error*, as his great spiritual crisis. Struck dumb while lecturing to his students, Ghazzâlî fell ill and gradually came to realize that his affliction was spiritual in nature: He had devoted himself to religious studies in hope of worldly fame and success rather than out of pure love of God. Consequently he gave up his position at the Niẓâmiyya and moved from Baghdad to Damascus (where, probably not coincidentally, Tutush's supporters were strong). From 488/1095 to 499/1105 Ghazzâlî lived in private retreat, often working at menial jobs, writing, and spending time in contemplation and learning from various Sufis still more about a life of asceticism and mysticism. In addition to his stay in Damascus, he performed the pilgrimage to Mecca and visited Jerusalem, Hebron, the Hijaz, and Egypt.

Around 499/1105, shortly after the death of Barkyârûq, Ghazzâlî returned to public life, accepting a post at the Niẓâmiyya Madrasa in Nishapur, where he had previously studied with Juvaynî. He later took charge of a madrasa and a Sufi retreat (*khânqâh*) near his native city of Ṭûs. It was there that he died in the year 505/1111.

Ghazzâlî is reputed to have written an enormous number of books.[2] Some of the works ascribed to him were merely brief epistles; others were duplicates of works known under variant titles; still others were incorrectly attributed to Ghazzâlî or were outright forgeries. Nonetheless, the corpus of his authentic works, many of which are still extant, included about seventy books dealing with such subjects as Islamic law and legal theory (*fiqh*), the theoretical and the practical aspects of Sufism, critiques of philosophy and theology, polemical tracts, and discussions of ethics and politics.[3]

---

[2] The corpus of writings attributed to Ghazzâlî has been surveyed and arranged in the probable sequence of composition by Maurice Bouyges (edited and revised after his death by M. Allard), *Essai de chronologie des oeuvres de al-Ghazali* (Beirut, 1959). See also G. Hourani, "The Chronology of Ghazâlî's Writings," *Journal of the American Oriental Society* 79(1959):225-33.

[3] An excellent representative sampling of Ghazzâlî's various writings in English translation may be found in R. McCarthy, *Freedom and Fulfillment* (Boston, 1980).

All of Ghazzâlî's writings are of great merit and interest, but there are three particularly important works on which his reputation primarily rests. First of all, there is his quasi-autobiographical treatise, *The Deliverance from Error* (*al-Munqidh min al-ḍalâl*),[4] a work often compared to St. Augustine's *Confessions* but quite unique in Islamic literature. In it, Ghazzâlî not only recounts the spiritual crisis he experienced in Baghdad (discussed above) but goes on to describe his subsequent search for a truth that would transcend all question and doubt. In doing so, he provides concise and remarkably clear descriptions of the major religio-intellectual trends of his day and his critiques or appreciations of each. As an introduction to the main features of Ghazzâlî's thought, it remains unexcelled. The basic concepts outlined in *The Deliverance from Error* are developed fully in two other texts. *The Incoherence of Philosophy* (*Tahâfut al-falâsifa*), written while Ghazzâlî was teaching in Baghdad, is a thorough and rather merciless criticism from a Muslim perspective of the aims, methods, and conclusions of Hellenistic-style philosophy.[5] *The Revival of the Religious Sciences* (*Iḥyâ' ᶜulûm al-din*), undoubtedly Ghazzâlî's greatest work, is well described as "a complete guide for the devout Muslim to every aspect of the religious life."[6] It offers a Muslim theory of knowledge,

---

[4] Available in a good English translation by W. Montgomery Watt, *The Faith and Practice of al-Ghazâlî* (London, 1953); it is also found in McCarthy's *Freedom and Fulfillment*.

[5] The *Tahâfut al-falâsifa* (edited by M. Bouyges; Beirut, 1927). There is an English translation by S. A. Kamali, *Al-Ghazali's Tahafut al-falasifa: Incoherence of the Philosophers*. Lahore, 1963.

[6] W. Montgomery Watt, "al-Ghazâlî," *Encyclopaedia of Islam* (new edition; Leiden, in progress), 2:1040. The *Iḥyâ'* has been published many times, but it is an immense work and there is no satisfactory complete translation of it into English. Many of its individual sections, however, have been translated; see the bibliography at the end of this work.

followed by detailed guidance on matters of faith, ritual, daily life, virtues and vices, and the mystical experience of God.

To understand the significance and influence of these and other works by Ghazzâlî, it is necessary to consider the milieu in which they were created.

The Historical Setting

The period of Ghazzâlî's life, 1058-1111, coincided with a very momentous epoch in the history of the Islamic world, which was in turmoil politically, religiously, and intellectually. As a result, Ghazzâlî's ideas cannot be fully appreciated without some reference to the historical environment which helped to shape them and which they, in turn, may have helped to alter.

Of the various events which occurred during Ghazzâlî's lifetime, the one which would most likely be familiar to a Western, non-Muslim, reader would certainly be the First Crusade. Ghazzâlî's departure from Baghdad occurred just as the call for a crusading movement was reaching its climax in Europe, and he may actually have been residing in Damascus when Jerusalem fell to the Crusaders in 1099. Yet these events had little discernable effect on Ghazzâlî's thought. This is probably due to the fact that in his time most Muslims viewed the Crusades as no more than a minor disruption on the periphery of the Islamic world; it was not until much later that they were regarded as of sufficient magnitude to be a cause for alarm. Ghazzâlî made only passing references to the idea of holy war (*jihâd*) in his works, and then usually in the context of spiritual endeavor, not actual physical struggle against rival religions or infidels. While one anti-Christian polemical tract has been attributed to him, it is little more than a typical

Muslim critique of the belief in the divinity of Christ.[7] For the most part, Ghazzâlî seems to have been genuinely interested in and favorably impressed by what he knew of Christianity, especially its ethical thought. In *The Alchemy of Happiness* and other writings, he frequently cites material about Jesus found in Christian texts to support his arguments and even quotes from the gospels. In short, Ghazzâlî's writing is remarkably free of the jaundiced communalism which the Crusades helped introduce into Muslim-Christian relations.

For Ghazzâlî and his contemporaries a far more spectacular and urgent political issue than the Crusades was the bitter sectarian struggle within the Muslim world between the Sunni Abbasid caliphate, with its capital in Iraq, and the rival Fatimid Shi'ite rulers based in Egypt. Ever since the death of the Prophet Muḥammad, there had been a general consensus among Muslims that there should continue to be one charismatic leader of the entire Muslim community, variously known as the caliph or "successor" of the Prophet (*khalîfat rasûl allâh*), the "deputy of God" (*khalîfat allâh*) the "commander of the faithful" (*amîr al-mu'minîn*), or the "authoritative leader" (*imâm*). However, there had been profound and sometimes violent conflicts over who was entitled to hold this office and what its actual powers should be. After a period of rule by four close associates of Muḥammad (three of whom were assassinated), the office was held by various members of a clan known as the Umayyads (41-132/661-750). Although in many ways quite successful, these rulers were widely regarded by Muslims as little more than secular kings, or even as illegitimate usurpers, since they had seized the caliphate by force and in earlier times their clan

---

[7] The *Radd al-jamîl ᶜalâ sarîḥ al-injîl*, edited and translated by R. Chidiac, *Réfutation excellente de la divinité de Jésus Christ d'après les Evangiles* (Paris, 1939).

had been notorious for its opposition to the Prophet Muḥammad and his religion. In 132/750, they were replaced by the Abbasid dynasty of caliphs, who had come to power as the result of a great revolutionary upheaval in the eastern areas of the Islamic world. Using their kinship with the Prophet Muḥammad (as descendants of his uncle al-ᶜAbbâs) to bolster their claims to charismatic authority, they sought to exercise absolutist power over the whole Islamic empire and to intrude on all aspects of Muslim life. Probably for this reason, the early Abbasids were instrumental in promoting the development of formal "schools" of Islamic law, but the legal scholars struggled to preserve their autonomy and finally became more or less independent of state control. Several of the Abbasid rulers, notably the caliphs al-Ma'mûn (198-218/813-33) and al-Muᶜtaṣim (218-27/833-42), attempted to assert authority over the religious life of their subjects by enforcing theological uniformity through an inquisition known as the *miḥna*, but that also ended in failure. Politically, their absolutism was more successful, but less than a century after the dynasty was established, even that power also began to erode. Soon, the Abbasid caliphs were little more than figureheads, real power being held by various local dynasties which usually professed loyalty to the Abbasids, primarily as a way of legitimizing their own right to rule over the Muslims. In Ghazzâlî's time, it was a dynasty of Turkish and Central Asian origin, the Seljuks (429-552/1038-1157), whose rulers (*sulṭâns*) both championed and dominated the Abbasid caliphate, having conquered the capital, Baghdad, in 447/1055.

The dynasty of the Fatimids (297-567/909-1171) also came to power after a kind of revolutionary movement strikingly similar in form to that which had installed the Abbasids. Although the Abbasids had once used their indirect kinship with the prophet to legitimize their caliphate, the Fatimids made the more specifically Shiʿite argument that their right to rule was based on direct descent from Muḥammad through his daughter Fâṭima, who had married Muḥammad's cousin and son-in-law, ᶜAlî. As such they claimed to be Shiʿite imâms, the only legitimate rulers in the Islamic world as well as infallible authorities on all religious and secular matters. Under circumstances which are still historically obscure, this straightforward doctrine of political legitimism was combined with a subtle and highly esoteric religious ideology to produce a revolutionary movement which, drawing on the strength of Berber tribal recruits, seized power in North Africa and installed one ᶜUbaydallah al-Mahdî as the first Fatimid caliph (proclaimed publicly in 297/910). In both religious and political terms, the absolutism of the Fatimid caliphs was far more complete and their ideology far more coherent than that of their Abbasid counterparts. After conquering Egypt in 358/969, they established various centers of learning, including the Aẓhar "university," to propagate their brand of Shiʿism and to train missionaries to preach on their behalf throughout the Muslim world. In the very year Ghazzâlî began teaching in Baghdad, one of the most famous of the pro-Fatimid activists, Ḥassân-e Ṣabbâḥ, seized the fortress of Alamût in northwestern Iran and attempted to advance the Fatimid cause through political assassinations of its chief opponents. His fanatical followers, popularly known as the Assassins, were thought to be responsible for the murder of the minister Niẓâm al-Mulk and other prominent pro-Abbasid leaders. The Abbasid-Fatimid conflict thus involved many issues—theological, legal, political, economic, social, cultural, and geographic—and amounted to an all out contest for domination over the heartlands of the Muslim world.

Since the Abbasids had long since lost any real political power, the task of defending them and the cause of Sunni

Islam was taken up by various eastern dynasties, mostly of Turkish origin. In particular, the Seljuk dynasty enthusiastically endorsed the anti-Fatimid campaign. They worked against the Fatimids on both the military and the ideological fronts. It is likely, for example, that the Seljuk minister Niẓâm al-Mulk decided to patronize the madrasa institution, and also founded the Niẓâmiyya Madrasa at which Ghazzâlî taught in Baghdad, in order to help counteract Fatimid propaganda. Although the Seljuks managed to oust Fatimid and pro-Fatimid forces from Syria, the invasion of Egypt which they apparently contemplated never materialized.

In the end, it was an intellectual as much as a military counter-offensive which turned the tide against the Fatimids, and in that effort Ghazzâlî played an important role by vigorously attacking the ideological underpinnings of the Fatimid cause, both at the political and the religious level. In theory, Ghazzâlî, rather like St. Augustine, seems to have viewed any state authority as little more than a necessary evil which should be avoided if at all possible by the pious. The circumstances of his time, however, led him to defend the practical necessity and legitimacy of the Abbasid caliphate against the Fatimids. To an extent, his writings on this subject were simply restatements of traditional Sunni arguments. Ghazzâlî, however, was too intelligent not to be aware of the irony inherent in championing the cause of a Sunni caliphate which was in actuality powerless. He thus began to develop the much more original and significant, as well as realistic, idea that the sultanate was also a legitimate institution and should be supported since it served to maintain the Sunni political and social order. As he says in one often quoted passage, "We consider that the function of the caliphate is contractually assumed by that member of the Abbasid house who is charged with it, and that the function of government in the various lands is carried out by sultans, who owe allegiance to the caliphs... Government in these days is a consequence solely of military power, and whosoever he may be to whom the holder of military power gives his allegiance, that person is the caliph."[8] His arguments had the important effect of giving theoretical legitimacy and ideological support to what was the *de facto* political situation in the Sunni world.[9]

The Religious and Intellectual Milieu

Behind the political and military duel of the Fatimids and Seljuks, there also lay a profound religious and intellectual ferment. Even at the time Ghazzâlî was born, more than four centuries after the death of the Prophet Muḥammad, Islam itself was in many ways still in the process of being elaborated as a coherent religious system. Broadly speaking, five general trends had established themselves in this regard, and the proponents of each were competing vigorously for the allegiance of Muslim rulers and/or the Muslim masses. These five trends or tendencies may, for convenience, be labelled

---

[8] In the *Revivification*, 2:124; cited by H. A. R. Gibb, "The Sunni Theory of the Caliphate," *Archives d'Histoire du Droit Oriental* 3(1939):402.

[9] Ghazzâlî's political ideas were developed in the *Mustaẓhirî* (an early defense of the Abbasid caliphate dedicated to the reigning caliph al-Mustaẓhir) and the *Golden Mean in Belief* (*al-Iqtiṣâd fi'l-iᶜtiqâd*; edited Ankara, 1962). His most detailed discourse on the nature of kingship was in a Persian work of the *fürstenspiegel* genre dedicated to a Seljuk prince, the *Nasîḥat al-mulûk*; translated by F. R. C. Bagley, *Ghazâlî's Book of Counsel for Kings* (Oxford, 1964). The same work exists in an Arabic version, the *The Smelted Ore* (*al-Tibr al-masbûk*). Another political treatise, *The Mystery of the Two Worlds* (*Sirr al-ᶜâlamayn wa kashf mâ fi'l-dârayn*) has probably been attributed in error to Ghazzâlî. For an excellent survey of his political thought, see Ann Lambton, *State and Government in Medieval Islam* (Oxford, 1981), pp. 107-29; also Henri Laoust, *La Politique de Gazâli* (Paris, 1970).

traditionist legalism, metaphysical philosophy, rational theology, esoteric (*bâṭinî*) Shi'ism, and Sufi mysticism.

Traditionist legalism had as its goal the elaboration of a comprehensive system of holy law which would enable the Muslim to fulfill the duty of worshipping God and living as He intended. This law was based primarily on the careful study of the explicit commands provided through divine revelation in the Koran and supplemented by prophetic example in the *ḥadîth* (orally transmitted traditions or reports of things the Prophet Muḥammad had said or done), but it could also be derived with the help of certain rigorous and systematically applied juristic methods (*fiqh*). The totality of this holy law constituted the *sharîᶜa*, a comprehensive body of rules to regulate virtually every aspect of Muslim life, whether public or private, religious or temporal. By the end of the third/ninth century, four "schools" of law (*madhhabs*), which survive to the present day, had crystallized around the teachings of four prominent legal scholars, for whom they were named: the Mâlikîs, Shâfiᶜîs, Ḥanafîs, and Ḥanbalîs.[10] Although these four great branches of Sunni Islam varied greatly in attitude—from the puritanical and literalist populism of the Ḥanbalîs to the liberal and pragmatic, often state-oriented Ḥanafîs—they were remarkably uniform in their actual expression of a comprehensive code of holy law. In many ways, this idealization of an Islamic nomocracy through the formulation of the sharîᶜa was the central concern and greatest achievement of classical Islamic civilization.

Ghazzâlî himself, as noted above, was involved in this enterprise and first distinguished himself in the study of fiqh.

---

[10] On Islamic law and its formulation, see Joseph Schacht, *The Origins of Muhammadan Jurisprudence* (Oxford, 1950) and *An Introduction to Islamic Law* (Oxford, 1964); N. J. Coulson, *A History of Islamic Law* (Edinburgh, 1964).

Throughout his work, it is obvious that few things disturbed him more than any antinomian tendency which would lead to disregard of the sharîᶜa. Although the *ᶜulamâ'*, the group of religious scholars responsible for expressing, guarding, and implementing the sharîᶜa, enjoyed considerable popular support and moral authority (at least in the major urban areas of the Muslim world),[11] Ghazzâlî was well aware of their potential vulnerabilities. He saw, for example, that there was sometimes a hypocritical disparity between the worldly life style of some of the scholars of the religious law and the demands of the code of pious conduct they taught; indeed, he had noted and worried about this tendency in his own life. Moreover, if the law was regarded simply as a set of intricate rules and regulations accepted on the basis of scholarly authority, without a firm foundation of faith and spirituality, it might appear terribly cold, austere, and empty to many ordinary Muslims. Ghazzâlî thus had no quarrel with the importance of the holy law in Islam; he simply recognized that taken alone it could easily seem spiritually incomplete and intellectually unconvincing.

One way in which some Muslims sought to fill precisely this kind of void was through metaphysical philosophy. Works of

---

[11] The ᶜulamâ' were uniquely positioned to influence the Muslim populace. As legal authorities, they were involved in numerous matters pertaining to daily life (business transactions, marriage contracts, etc.). They dominated private education and religious instruction, both in the home and in the mosque. The Koran and the traditions were also easily accessible to the masses, even those who were illiterate, since the Koran was frequently memorized and recited and oral transmission of traditions was a common activity. This facilitated popular appreciation of the ᶜulamâ's command of these fields of knowledge, and we hear of huge crowds coming to hear famous scholars teach about the Koran and the ḥadîth. These points are brought out fairly well in Munir-ud-Din Ahmad, *Muslim Education and the Scholars' Social Status up to the 5th Century Muslim Era* (Zurich, 1968).

Greek philosophy, mostly of a late Hellenistic Aristotelian and neo-Platonic character, had been translated into Arabic and were being championed and developed by a number of famous Muslim philosophers: al-Kindî (d. 252/866); al-Fârâbî (d. 339/950); and especially Ghazzâlî's great contemporary Ibn Sînâ (known in the West as Avicenna; d. 428/1037).[12] Ghazzâlî saw this tendency as a positive danger to the Muslim community and attempted to discredit it in two major works, *The Intentions of the Philosophers* (*Maqâsid al-falâsifa*) and *The Incoherence of Philosophy* (*Tahâfut al-falâsifa*); his findings were also summarized in his *Deliverance from Error*.[13] While he admitted that philosophy had produced much of value that should not be rejected out of hand, particularly logic and the mathematical sciences, he argued that it also held up as certain knowledge what were really nothing more than opinions. Worse, many of these ideas conflicted with the religion of Islam and led to outright heresy. On three crucial points, all derived ultimately from Aristotle, Ghazzâlî held that the philosophers were not only wrong but so irreligious that they were really infidels (that is, they had forfeited their status as Muslims). These points were (1) the concept of the eternity of the world as opposed to the creation *ex nihilo* of revelation; (2) the concept that God knows only universals not particulars as opposed to the personal God of the Koran who is "closer than one's jugular vein" and is aware of all that happens; and (3) the

---

[12] On this subject, see Majid Fakhri, *A History of Islamic Philosophy* (second edition; London, 1983); De Lacy O'Leary, *Arabic Thought and Its Place in History* (London, 1939); T. J. DeBoer, *The History of Philosophy in Islam* (London, 1903).

[13] *The Intentions of the Philosophers* (*Maqâṣid al-falâsifa*; ed. Cairo, 1331/1915-16); for the *Tahâfut*, see above n. 5. While critical of many of the teachings of the philosophers, he did not reject all their methods; he explained and justified the use of logic in works such as the *The Standard for Knowledge* (*Miʿyâr al-ʿilm*) and *The Just Balance* (*al-Qisṭâs al-mustaqîm*).

denial of the resurrection of the body in direct contradiction to Koranic doctrine. It is not necessary here to describe the many complicated Ghazzâlî arguments developed to rebut these notions. As a practical matter, it was sufficient for him to bring to public attention the fundamental conflict of the teachings of the philosophers with Koranic doctrines. The cause of the philosophers against Ghazzâlî was not helped by their frequent arrogance, elitism, and antinomianism, as when Ibn Sînâ taught that the soul of the philosopher was superior to the soul of an ordinary person or that the philosopher, being superior to the prophet by virtue of greater understanding, was freed from the bonds of the holy law that applied to common people.[14] However convincing or unconvincing Ghazzâlî's critique may have been to later philosophers,[15] there is no doubt that in the court of Muslim popular opinion it prevailed, forever altering the intellectual climate of the Islamic world.

The trend represented by the study of rational theology (*kalâm*) was similar to that of philosophy except that it wanted to use reason in defense of a religious framework, not as an end in itself. In the early centuries of Islam, a purely rationalist theology known as Mu^ctazilism had been a powerful movement, at times backed by the Abbasid government. Mu^ctazilî theologians had emphasized the importance of correct belief and utilized the concepts and methodology of philosophy to concentrate on the formulation of doctrine. In this they emphasized that in discussing the attributes of God

---

[14] Ibn Sînâ and Fârâbî are singled out for criticism of this sort in the *Deliverance*; see Watt, *Faith and Practice*, pp. 72-73. An English translation of some of the passages that Ghazzâlî would probably have regarded as offensive may be found in A. J. Arberry, *Avicenna on Theology* (London, 1951), especially pp. 9-24, 64-76.

[15] The best known attempt by a Muslim philosopher to rebut Ghazzâlî was by Ibn Rushd (Averroes); see Simon van den Bergh, *Averroes' Tahafut al-Tahafut (The Incoherence of the Incoherence)* (London, 1969).

any form of anthropomorphism had to be rejected (even if this meant making allegorical interpretations of certain Koranic verses); that God's justice necessarily limited his power and endowed humans with free will; and that "God's speech" (the Koran) was created rather than eternal. The Muslim community, especially those most concerned with the primacy of traditionist legalism, were uncomfortable with these teachings and even more disturbed by the fact that they were being imposed with the help of state power.

By Ghazzâlî's time, this form of theology had been decisively rejected in favor of a dogmatic theology known as Ashᶜarism.[16] Its founder, Abu'l-Ḥasan al-Ashᶜarî (d. 324/935-36), frowned on any purely speculative theology and consequently rejected almost every teaching of the Muᶜtazilites. In keeping with a more literal reading of scripture and tradition ("without asking how"), he accepted the Koranic attributes of God while denying that they implied anthropomorphism; held that the Koran was the uncreated Word of God; and insisted on the primacy of God's omnipotence even if that required belief in predestination. Al-Ashᶜarî's goal was clearly to harmonize this type of theology with traditionist legalism, and it should be noted that Ghazzâlî's teacher, Juvaynî, was an eminent authority in both fields and so, to an extent, was Ghazzâlî himself. But the alliance was an uneasy one. While the theologians professed to admire the legal scholars and sought, unsuccessfully, to have legal and theological training combined in the curriculum of the madrasas, they often viewed traditional and popular religion with disdain. The legal scholars suspected that the

---

[16] On which, see R. C. McCarthy (ed. and tr.), *The Theology of al-Ashᶜarî* (Beirut, 1953); A. S. Tritton, *Muslim Theology* (London, 1947), pp. 166-74; George Makdisi, "Ash'arî and the Ash'arites in Islamic Religious History," *Studia Islamica* 17(1962):37-80 and 18(1963):19-39.

theologians were still overly influenced by the methods of non-Islamic philosophy, were dangerously close to allowing reason to supplant reliance on revelation and prophetic tradition, and were all too eager to co-operate with the authorities of the state in enforcing doctrinal conformity.

Ghazzâlî certainly became aware of the limitations of theology and began to distance himself from it. In *The Deliverance from Error*, he noted that theology, like logic in philosophy, was a useful tool, but neither an end in itself nor a path to certain knowledge. Above all, it was no more appropriate to base matters of faith on the blind acceptance of authoritative theologians than it was to limit knowledge of the holy law to mere imitation of the legal experts: "Whoever claims that theology, abstract proofs, and systematic classification are the foundation of belief is an innovator. Rather is belief a light which God bestows on the hearts of His creatures as the gift and bounty from Him, sometimes through an explainable conviction from within, sometimes because of a dream in sleep, sometimes by seeing the state of bliss of a pious man and the transmission of his light through association and conversation with him, sometimes through one's own state of bliss."[17] He was also appalled by the intolerance and exclusivity of some theologians as seen in their readiness to demean the simple faith of others: "Among the most extreme and extravagant of men are a group of scholastic theologians who dismiss the Muslim common people as unbelievers and claim that whoever does not know scholastic theology in the form they recognize and does not know the prescriptions of the Holy Law according to the proofs which they have adduced is

---

17 In *The Decisive Criterion for Distinguishing Islam and Unbelief* (*al-Fayṣal al-tafriqa bayn al-islâm wa'l-zandaqa*; ed. Cairo, 1381/1961), p. 202; translated by Bernard Lewis, *Islam* (New York, 1974), 2:20-21.

an unbeliever."[18] It is perhaps revealing that one of Ghazzâlî's very last writings warned of the dangers of exposing ordinary believers to any form of kalâm.[19]

Shi'ism in Islam is a very complex phenomenon about which it is difficult and dangerous to generalize.[20] The term is applied to a multitude of movements ranging from extremely heterodox and politically revolutionary sects to branches of Islam which are barely distinguishable from those regarded as mainstream or Sunni in character. About the only feature the various forms of Shi'ism have in common is that they substitute some charismatic leader, usually called an imâm, believed to have been designated as such by God and further distinguished by some degree of kinship to Muḥammad, for the various caliphs recognized by Sunni Muslims.

In Ghazzâlî's time, by far the most powerful form of Shi'ism was that espoused by the Fatimids, known as Ismâᶜîlî or "Sevener" Shi'ism.[21] Although this went through its own process of evolution, it generally taught (1) that Islam had a concealed, inner, esoteric dimension (the *bâṭin*, often linked to a cosmology of strikingly neo-Platonic terminology) that was

---

[18] Ibid.

[19] *The Restraining of Commoners from the Science of Theology* (*Iljâm al-ᶜawâmm ᶜan ᶜilm al-kalâm*; ed. Cairo, 1351/1932).

[20] Two general works on this subject are Moojan Momen, *An Introduction to Shi'i Islam* (Oxford, 1985) and S. H. M. Jafri, *The Origins and Early Development of Shi'a Islam* (London, 1979). Unfortunately, the former is slanted towards coverage of Twelver Shi'ism and periods later than Ghazzâlî, while the latter deals only with the very early historical development of Shi'ism.

[21] Scholarship on the type of Fatimid Shi'ism which would have been familiar to Ghazzâlî is still in its preliminary stages of development. For two radically different interpretations of one aspect of it, see M. G. S. Hodgson, *The Order of Assassins* (The Hague, 1955) and B. Lewis, *The Origins of Ismâᶜîlism* (Cambridge, 1940). A new and important general work on this type of Shi'ism is Farhad Daftari, *The Isma'ilis: Their History and Development* (Cambridge, 1990).

far more important than its literal and outward aspects (the *ẓâhir*), (2) that the ordinary believer had to be gradually initiated into an understanding of the bâṭin, (3) that for this he absolutely required authoritative guidance from an infallible imâm who was divinely entrusted with knowledge of the deepest secrets of the faith, (4) that these imâms had appeared in cycles of seven going back to Adam, each seventh imâm bringing a new revelation to supplant that of his predecessors, and that this would continue until a future imâm, the Qâ'im, propagated a final and perfect revelation of the bâṭin; (5) that in its current phase the imâmate belonged to the lineage of the seventh Shi'ite imâm, Ismâᶜîl b. Jaᶜfar al-Ṣâdiq, reputed ancestor of the Fatimid caliphs, and (6) that the authority of certain imâms thus extended even to the point of abrogating Koranic revelation and prophetic tradition, rendering the holy law and obedience to it redundant.

If Ghazzâlî was ever vehement about anything, it was in his rejection of this system of thought, which he felt was as dangerous as it was unconvincing. He derisively referred to its adherents as *bâṭinî*s (owing to their fascination with religious obscurities) and *taᶜlîmî*s (misguided and gullible people who allowed reliance on a supposedly infallible imâm to substitute for real spiritual understanding). As he noted in the *Deliverance*, insofar as anyone needed an infallible instructor, that need had already been fulfilled by the Prophet Muḥammad. Beyond that, the bâṭinîs themselves could not always agree on who such an infallible teacher might be or claimed that he was "hidden." Finally, most of what these supposedly infallible teachers produced seemed to Ghazzâlî little more than half-baked Pythagoreanism which he regarded as "the dregs of philosophy."[22]

---

[22] See Watt, *Faith and Practice*, pp. 43-54 for the appropriate passages from the *Deliverance*. Ghazzâlî provided more sustained critiques of this type of

As diverse as these four strands of Islamic thought were, they all were ultimately based on a similar conception of the religion: a creed, doctrine, or practice formulated and guarded by an intellectual elite and passively accepted and followed by the masses of ordinary believers. It is easy to see how Ghazzâlî would worry that even something as fundamental as ritual might become merely mechanical and soulless under the weight of such a system. It was for this reason that he developed a strong interest in the fifth great trend manifesting itself in Muslim society, that of Islamic mysticism or Sufism (*taṣawwuf*).

Sufism represented more an attitude and a way of life than a school of thought.[23] Its practitioners, the Sufis (from *ṣûfî*, a word of uncertain etymology), had been active from the earliest periods of Islamic history. Their mysticism was of necessity intensely personal and individualistic and therefore diverse in its specific expressions. At heart, however, most of them were motivated by two primary factors: the desire to attain direct knowledge (*maʿrifa*) of God and the wish to live the kind of life that would enable them to do so. They emphasized the importance of asceticism, of sincere piety, of self-purification, of acting out of a genuine love of God rather than a sometimes hypocritical subservience to the holy law out

---

Shi'ism in the *Mustaẓhirî* or *Infamies of the Bâṭinîs* (*Faḍâ'iḥ al-bâṭiniyya wa faḍâ'il al-mustaẓhiriyya*; ed. Cairo, 1964); the *Just Balance* (*al-Qisṭâs al-mustaqîm*); and the *Decisive Criterion* (*Fayṣal al-tafriqa*). I. Goldziher, *Streitschrift des Gazâlî gegen die Bâṭinijja-Sekte* (Leiden, 1916) gives an abridged translation of the *Qisṭâs*; there are also excerpts from these works in McCarthy, *Freedom and Fulfillment*, pp. 145-74 (the *Fayṣal*), 175-286 (the *Faḍâ'iḥ*), and 287-332 (the *Qisṭâs*).

[23] For an introduction to the vast subject of Sufism, see Annemarie Schimmel, *Mystical Dimensions of Islam* (Chapel Hill, 1975) which provides an extensive bibliography.

of fear. They also clearly believed that each individual was capable of some direct experience of God (or even union with Him), independent of any transmitted revelation, authoritative teaching, or intellectual exercise. People who attained this goal were regarded as "friends of God" and often idolized as saints and miracle-workers by the masses. Many began to act as spiritual guides (*murshid*s or *pîr*s) to assist others in the mystic journey towards God. They often espoused unconventional methods for achieving this intensely personal, passionate, and ecstatic condition and described the mystical experience with poetical metaphors praising intoxication and eroticism. Some of their ceremonies and practices, such as various forms of *dhikr* (group meetings for songs, dances, or chants, often including both men and women, Muslims and non-Muslims together) or the visitation of the tombs of saints, were at variance with the established rituals and practices of formal Islam. Occasionally, mystics claimed to have reached an actual union with God and in their exuberance made no secret of their disregard for conventional religious practice and law. One of the most famous and popular of the mystics, al-Ḥallâj, was executed in 309/922 on just such charges of blasphemy.[24]

The circumstances surrounding the martyrdom of al-Ḥallâj showed that Sufism was immensely appealing as a popular form of religion, but that it could also arouse the animosity of theologians, bâṭinî ideologues, and some members of the traditionist/legal establishment. The Shi'ites were particularly hostile to the Sufis because the substitution of personal experience and a host of "friends of God" for the charisma of a

[24] Al-Ḥallâj is the subject of one of the greatest works of Islamic scholarship, Louis Massignon's *La Passion de Ḥusayn Ibn Manṣûr Ḥallâj* (second edition; Paris, 1975); now available in an English translation by Herbert Mason, *The Passion of al-Hallâj, Mystic and Martyr of Islam* (Princeton, 1982).

unique, sinless, infallible imâm struck at the very heart of their system of belief. Most theologians instinctively distrusted any popular expression of religion, particularly one as anti-intellectual as Sufism could be (expressed in the slogan "break the inkpots and tear up the books"). The attitude of the legal scholars was ambivalent. They were not necessarily opposed to mysticism as such (many were privately Sufis themselves), but they realized that Sufism, by encouraging unconventional additions to Muslim ritual and tolerating ecstatic practices, could conflict with the holy law.[25] They also saw that Sufism provided convenient shelter for any number of eccentrics and charlatans whose behavior would normally be objectionable.

Ghazzâlî's genius lay in recognizing that Sufism, with its great popular appeal, could be an invaluable support to Sunni legalism against free-thinking philosophy and bâṭinî Shi'ism. To that end, he worked to give Sufism its own rigorously Islamic intellectual framework and to contain or redirect its pantheistic and antinomian tendencies. As he argued in *The Deliverance from Error*, his study of Sufism had convinced him "with certainty that it is above all the mystics who walk on the road of God; their life is the best life, their method the soundest method, their character the purest character."[26] The superiority of the mystics arose (1) from the fact that their knowledge was not derived as in other systems but based on immediate experience (*dhawq*) and was thus incontestable and (2) they

---

[25] George Makdisi has pointed out that the antipathy of some traditionists towards Sufism has been exaggerated; see his "L'Islam Hanbalisant," *Revue des Études Islamiques* 43(1975):45-76. However, there is a deep suspicion of it even today among some of the more conservative and legalistic religious scholars; R. Caspar "La Mystique Musulmane: recherches et tendences," *Revue de l'Institut des Belles Lettres Arabes (Tunis)* 25(1962), p. 289 n. 34 quotes an authority from the Azhar Islamic University in Cairo as saying that "the great majority of those whom the orientalists call Muslim mystics have nothing in common with Islam."

[26] As translated in Watt, *Faith and Practice*, p. 60.

were not just "men of words" but rather of purity and action whose every step was guided by "the lamp of prophetic revelation." The true mystic might attain to an indescribable absorption in God (*fanâ'*), but not to a pantheistic union or connection with him. Above all, the true mystic would realize that any sin was a "deadly poison": No real mystic would think his knowledge of mysticism elevated him above the duties of worship or the requirements of the law.[27] Ghazzâlî consistently strived for a Sufism based on sober piety and masterfully buttressed the outward teachings of the law with the deep inner spirituality of the mystic. This insistence on the natural harmony of Sufism and the law pervades all of Ghazzâlî's finest writings and marks his greatest contribution to Islamic thought.

Ghazzâlî's Influence and Significance

In the history of Islamic civilization, Ghazzâlî can best be understood as a great reconciler of the diverse trends of thought just discussed. Although in a sense he attacked and discredited the philosophers and the bâṭinî Shi'ites, and diluted the importance of the theologians, he also incorporated some of their best ideas into his own work. He certainly did not shy away from use of logic and rational argument in defense of religion, from looking for the deep inner meanings in religious texts and practices, or even from employing metaphorical

[27] Ghazzâlî's most direct criticism of radically antinomian tendencies of this type was in a work on people he called "Latitudinarians" (*ibâḥiyya*); the tract has been translated by Otto Pretzl, *Die Streitschrift des Gazâlî gegen die Ibâhîja*, Munich, 1933. His comments on the ecstatic state found in the *Alchemy* (below, Chapter Six) show that he had a broad tolerance for the eccentricities of the Sufis, but not to the point of disregard for the explicit requirements of the law.

interpretation of controversial Koranic verses.[28] To the dry study of the law, he added the warm and rich faith and deep spiritual understanding of the mystic; the ecstasy and enthusiasm of the mystic he tempered with the duty to know and obey God's commandments. He was thus able to sort out, prioritize, and synthesize the various religious tendencies of his time into a comprehensive religious system which has remained at the heart of mainstream Sunni Islam ever since.

In this, Ghazzâlî was certainly not free from critics, both in his lifetime and after his death. The Muslim philosophers, led by Ibn Rushd (Averroes; d. 595/1198) in his *Incoherence of the Incoherence* (*Tahâfut al-tahâfut*), sharply criticized Ghazzâlî for his attacks on philosophy and attempted to point out the many inconsistencies in his writing. The more conservative Muslim traditionists or literalists, notably Ibn al-Jawzî (d. 597/1200), accused Ghazzâlî of fabricating ḥadîth and concealing his actual esoteric beliefs behind a façade of piety; a few even called for his writings to be burned. Others, such as the very influential Ibn Taymiyya (d. 728/1328), did not necessarily attack Ghazzâlî directly but undermined some aspects of his work by denouncing various Sufi practices (which Ghazzâlî tended to tolerate) as dangerous innovations which the Muslim community should reject. But by far the overwhelming consensus among Muslims has been that Ghazzâlî was truly a "proof of Islam." As Tâj al-Dîn al-Subkî (d. 771/1370), a renowned Muslim jurist himself, put it, Ghazzâlî's "achievements and his fame have covered the earth and he who really knows his teaching knows that it goes beyond his fame... He taught at a time when people had more need of the truth than darkness has of the light of the heavens and the

---

[28] This will be apparent in his discussion of the "Throne" and "Chair" of God and the "Tablet of Destiny" in the *Alchemy of Happiness* itself, below, p. 18.

barren land of the fruitful rain... If there had been a prophet after Muḥammad, it surely would have been al-Ghazzâlî."[29]

Ghazzâlî's influence also extended well beyond the Arabo-Persian Islamic world. Parts of his work have since been translated into Turkish, Urdu, Pushto, Bengali, Malay, Hebrew, Latin, English, French, Italian, Spanish, German, and Russian, thus reaching a vastly larger Muslim and non-Muslim audience. Not only can his influence be traced in the thought of numerous Muslim mystics and pietists, it can be found in the works of Jewish philosophers and mystics such as Maimonedes, Alemanus, or Ibn Habib; among Eastern Christians like the Jacobite Bar Hebraeus; and in the writings of Europeans as diverse as Aquinas, Dante, and Pascal.[30]

The Alchemy of Happiness

There has been much confusion about the text in Persian by Ghazzâlî known as *The Alchemy of Happiness* (*Kîmîâ-yi sa*ᶜ*âdat*) and its relation to his magnum opus, *The Revivification of the Religious Sciences* (*Iḥyâ'* ᶜ*ulûm al-din*).[31] The confusion has not been helped by the fact that there is a treatise in Arabic with the same title.[32] The *Revivification*, written in

---

[29] In Subkî's *Ṭabaqât al-Shâfi*ᶜ*iyya al-kubrâ* 4:101-2; cited in Smith, *Ghazâlî*, p. 215.

[30] On Ghazzâlî's influence outside the Muslim world, especially through his concepts of Muḥammad's ascension to the seven heavens and the beatific vision, see Smith, *Ghazâlî*, pp. 198-226; also the more technical articles by S. de Beaurecueil, "Gazzâlî et S. Thomas d'Aquin," *Bulletin de l'Institut français d'archéologie orientale* 46(1947):199-238; M. Alonso, "Influencia de Algazel en el mundo latino," *Al-Andalus* 23(1958):371-80.

[31] See Bouyges, *Essai de Chronologie*, pp. 59-60 for discussion of the various views.

[32] See Bouyges, *Essai de Chronologie*, pp. 136-137. The Arabic treatise has been edited by Muḥammad ᶜAbd al-ᶜAlîm (Cairo, n. d.); it is actually an Arabic translation of part of the opening of the *Alchemy*.

Arabic, has naturally been Ghazzâlî's best known work in the Arab world and among Western scholars of Islam. The *Alchemy* has generally been the work most familiar to Persian speaking audiences in Iran and the Indian subcontinent. Since relatively few scholars were familiar with both texts, and the Persian text lacked a critical edition, it was variously maintained that the *Alchemy* was nothing more than a translation, or an abridged translation, of the *Revivification* or that it was an altogether different work. Now that the full Persian text has been published,[33] it is possible to clarify this issue.

In the introduction to the Persian text, Ghazzâlî explicitly states that he wrote the *Alchemy* as an epitome of the Arabic *Revivification* and some of his other writings, simplified and written in Persian in order to reach a broader, popular audience.[34] The *Revivification* and the *Alchemy* are thus very similar to each other, almost close enough to call the *Alchemy* a translation of the *Revivification*. Both are organized according to the same plan. They are divided into four major sections, each of which is subdivided into ten chapters. They deal, in sequence, with acts of worship, acts pertaining to everyday life, acts that lead to perdition, and acts that lead to salvation. With only a few exceptions, the arrangement of the forty chapters of the *Revivification* is identical to that of those of the *Alchemy*. (For a comparison of the *Revivication* and the *Alchemy*, see pages xxxix-xli.)

There are, however, some significant differences between the two works. While the preface to the *Revivification* simply outlines the proposed structure of the book and hammers

---

[33] A good recent edition is that by Ḥusayn Khadîv-jam (Tehran, 1361/1983).

[34] In the Khadîv-jam edition, 1:9, he explains that ordinary people (*ᶜavâmm-i khalq*) had requested a version of his ideas written in Persian in a way that would not exceed their comprehension.

home the point that it is intended as a guide to action rather than contemplation, the introduction to the *Alchemy* is much longer and more involved. It comprises four chapters, none of which are found in the *Revivification*, dealing with the theme of knowledge: knowledge of self, knowledge of God, knowledge of this world as it really is, and knowledge of the hereafter. Taken together, they offer an overview of Ghazzâlî's philosophy as a whole.

The specific contents of the individual chapters of the *Revivification* and the *Alchemy* are also somewhat different. The *Revivification*, for example, tends to make more extensive use of quotations from the Koran and citations of ḥadîth, while the *Alchemy* is somewhat more likely to use anecdotes from the lives of famous Sufis. The *Revivification* also tends to dwell at greater length on the external, legalistic aspects of religious practices while the *Alchemy* is somewhat freer in elaborating on their "inner" spiritual aspects.

Both the *Alchemy* and the *Revivification* have been attributed to the middle period of Ghazzâlî's literary career during his retreat from public life (from 488/1095 to 499/1105). The *Alchemy*, however, mentions several of Ghazzâlî's writings in addition to the *Revivification*, including the *Jawâhir al-qur'ân* (*Jewels of the Koran*), the *Maᶜânî asmâ' allâh al-ḥusnâ* (*Explication of the Names of God*), the *Bidâyat al-hidâya* (*Commencement of Guidance*), and the *Mishkât al-anwâr* (*Niche for Lights*). Since the *Mishkât* is a very late work by Ghazzâlî,[35] it would appear that the *Alchemy* should be dated to the final years of Ghazzâlî's life. It is thus particularly appropriate for a translation intended to acquaint a general

[35] See Bouyges, *Essai de Chronologie*, pp. 65-66; W. Gairdner, "Al-Ghazâlî's *Mishkât al-Anwâr* and the Ghazâlî-Problem," *Der Islam* 5(1914):133. The *Alchemy* text cites the complete form of the title of this work as found in the older Arabic manuscripts: *Mishkât al-anwâr wa miṣfât al-asrâr*.

modern audience with the ideas of this great Muslim intellectual, as it represents one of his last works, as well as a summation of his thought and an attempt to reach the broadest possible readership.

This collection of excerpts from the *Alchemy* is based on an English translation made by Claud Field in 1910. Just as an earlier translation of this work had been made from a Turkish text,[36] Field worked, unfortunately, from an uncritical Urdu version of the text rather than the original Persian. Despite this, Field's translation has two great merits: It renders the text in very felicitous, although pleasantly archaic, English prose, and it translates the whole of the four introductory chapters of the *Alchemy*, thus making available that section of the *Alchemy* which has no parallel in the *Revivification*.

For this revision of Field's translation, I have compared his text to the appropriate sections of the recently published Persian edition. In contrast to the Persian text, Field's translation is considerably condensed in parts as it omits various redundant phrases, traditions, and anecdotes cited in the Persian text. Generally speaking, the opening and closing parts of each chapter are very close to the Persian text, but the middle sections tend to be abbreviated, sometimes to as little as a third of their original size. All in all, however, Field's translation is faithful to the Persian original and certainly does no violence to the essence of Ghazzâlî's message.

I have therefore limited myself to making only minor changes to the Field translation. I have corrected its typographical errors and changed the spelling of names and terms to conform with an acceptable modern system for the transliteration of the Arabic script. I have also reorganized the sequence of some of the chapters and altered the division of a

---

[36] H. A. Homes, *The Alchemy of Happiness by M. al-Ghazzali the Mohammedan Philosopher* (Albany, 1873).

number of paragraphs to make them conform to that in the Persian edition of the *Alchemy*. Finally, Field's annotations to the text were both few and inadequate; I have therefore omitted them and substituted my own footnotes to identify the people and quotations mentioned in the text, to clarify any points which might prove puzzling to readers unfamiliar with Ghazzâlî and Islamic thought, and to note any major discrepancies between the translation and the published text.

In conclusion, I must make some apology for presuming to offer what is, after all, no more than a revision of an English translation of an Urdu abridgment of a Persian recension of a book first written in Arabic almost a thousand years ago. To my mind, there could hardly be better testimony to Ghazzâlî's universal appeal than this polyglot transmission of his writing. If, as I hope, the clarity and brilliance of his thought can survive so many layers of obfuscation to reach the modern reader, it is yet another testimony to the magnitude of his genius.

Elton L. Daniel

The Hârûniyya Mausoleum. Popularly regarded as the tomb of Hârûn al-Rashîd, this thirteenth century building is most likely a mausoleum built in honor of al-Ghazzâlî. It is located on the outskirts of Mashhad, Iran, near the ruins of medieval Ṭûs. (Photograph by E. L. Daniel)

A Comparison of Chapters in the *Revivification* and the *Alchemy*

Revivification of the Religious Sciences (Cairo Edition)	*The Alchemy of Happiness* (Khadîv-jam Edition)
Preface	Preface
	Introduction:
	1. On Knowledge of Self [1:13]
	2. On Knowledge of God [1:47]
	3. On Knowledge of this World [1:71]
	4. On Knowledge of the Hereafter [1:81]
Part I: Acts of Worship	Part I: Acts of Worship
1. Religious Science [1:4]	1. On Acquiring the Creed of the Sunnis [1:123]
2. The Articles of Faith [1:73]	2. On Religious Science [1:131]
3. The Mysteries of Ritual Purity [1:102]	3. On Ritual Purity [1:139]
4. The Mysteries of Ritual Prayer [1:117]	4. On Ritual Prayer [1:159]
5. The Mysteries of Required Charity [1:163]	5. On Required Charity [1:185]
6. The Mysteries of Fasting [1:181]	6. On Fasting [1:207]
7. The Mysteries of the Pilgrimage [1:187]	7. On Pilgrimage [1:218]

6. The Shame of Worldliness [3:151]	6. On Healing the Love of Money and the Plague of Avarice [2:149]
7. The Shame of Avarice and the Love of Wealth [3:184]	7. On Healing the Love of Status and Pomp [2:189]
8. The Shame of Love of Status and Hypocrisy [3:206]	8. On Healing Dissimulation and Religious Hypocrisy [2:207]
9. On the Shame of Pride and Vanity [3:255]	9. On Healing Pride and Vanity [2:247]
10. On the Shame of Deception [3:288]	10. On Healing Deception and Illusion [2:285]
Part IV: Acts that Assure Salvation	Part IV: Acts that Assure Salvation
1. On Repentance [4:2]	1. On Repentance [2:317]
2. On Patience and Gratitude [4:48]	2. On Patience and Gratitude [2:243]
3. On Fear and Hope [4:112]	3. On Fear and Hope [2:385]
4. On Poverty and Asceticism [4:148]	4. On Poverty and Asceticism [2:419]
5. On the Unity of God and Entrusting Oneself to Him [4:187]	5. On Truthfulness and Sincerity [2:453]
6. On Love and Desire [for God] [4:227]	6. On Introspection and Recollection [of God] [2:483]
7. On Intention, Sincerity, and Truthfulness [4:282]	7. On Meditation and Penitence [2:503]
8. On the Recollection [of God] and Introspection [4:306]	8. On Entrusting Oneself to God and His Unity [2:525]
9. On Meditation [4:331]	9. On Love and Desire [for God] [2:567]
10. On Death and the Hereafter [4:352]	10. On Death and the Hereafter [2:613]

the Alchemy of Happiness

Introduction

[The Persian text begins with the usual formula, "In the name of God, the Compassionate, the Merciful," which precedes virtually all works by Muslim authors. This is followed by a florid doxology, blessings on the Prophet Muḥammad, his family, and his companions, and a statement of the purpose and arrangement of the book. This is considerably abbreviated in Field's translation as follows:]

Know, O Beloved, that man was not created in jest or at random, but marvelously made and for some great end. Although he is not from everlasting, yet he lives for ever; and though his body is mean and earthly, yet his spirit is lofty and divine. When in the crucible of abstinence he is purged from carnal passions he attains to the highest, and in place of being a slave to lust and anger becomes endowed with angelic qualities. Attaining that state, he finds his heaven in the contemplation of Eternal Beauty, and no longer in fleshly delights. The spiritual alchemy which operates this change in him, like that which transmutes base metals into gold, is not easily discovered, nor to be found in the house of every old woman. It is to explain that alchemy and its methods of operation that the author has undertaken this work, which he has entitled, *The Alchemy of Happiness*. Now the treasuries of God, in which this alchemy is to be sought, are the hearts of the prophets, and he who seeks it elsewhere will be disappointed and bankrupt on the day of judgment when he hears the word,

"We have lifted the veil from off thee, and thy sight today is keen."[1]

God has sent on earth a hundred and twenty-four thousand prophets[2] to teach men the prescription of this alchemy, and how to purify their hearts from baser qualities in the crucible of abstinence. This alchemy may be briefly described as turning away from the world to God, and its constituents are four:

1. The knowledge of self.
2. The knowledge of God.
3. The knowledge of this world as it really is.
4. The knowledge of the next world as it really is.

We shall now proceed to expound these four constituents in order.

---

[1] Koran, 50:22.

[2] In Islam, there is a distinction between "apostles" (singular *rasûl*/plural *rusul*) who are the bearers of a "book" of revelation and "prophets" (*nabî/anbiyâ'*) who are simply inspired by the divine. Tradition held that there had been 124,000 prophets and 315 apostles. The Koran itself, however, identifies only nine apostles (notably Moses, Jesus, and Muḥammad) and twenty-eight prophets (such as Jacob, David, Elias, or John the Baptist).

Chapter One
Knowledge of Self

Knowledge of self is the key to the knowledge of God, according to the saying: "He who knows himself knows God,"[1] and, as it is written in the Koran, "We will show them Our signs in the world and in themselves, that the truth may be manifest to them."[2] Now nothing is nearer to thee than thyself, and if thou knowest not thyself how canst thou know anything else? If thou sayest "I know myself," meaning thy outward shape, body, face, limbs, and so forth, such knowledge can never be a key to the knowledge of God. Nor, if thy knowledge as to that which is within only extends so far, that when thou art hungry thou eatest, and when thou art angry thou attackest someone, wilt thou progress any further in this path, for the beasts are thy partners in this? But real self-

---

[1] This is supposed to be a *ḥadîth* (that is, a statement attributed to the Prophet Muḥammad; such sayings were verified by the study of the names of the various authorities reported to have been involved in the oral transmission of the tradition). This idea appears in many works attributed to al-Ghazzâlî: see Abdul Qayyum, *Letters of al-Ghazzali* (Lahore, 1976), p. 118, where he writes, "If you would know God, you must look into your own heart." Cf. the *Madnûn,* translated by A. Hazarvi, *The Mysteries of the Human Soul* (Lahore, 1981), p. 28.

[2] Koran, 41:53. This verse attracted much attention among both esoteric Shi'ites and certain Muslim mystics. It inspired the construction of elaborate parallels between the structure of the cosmos, the world, and the human body; for an example, see J. K. Birge, *The Bektashi Order of Dervishes* (London, 1937), pp. 239-243 and illustration #17. Note that Ghazzâlî distances himself from the notion that the physical body reveals anything about the nature or appearance of God.

knowledge consists in knowing the following things: What art thou in thyself, and from whence hast thou come? Whither art thou going, and for what purpose has thou come to tarry here awhile, and in what does thy real happiness and misery consist? Some of thy attributes are those of animals, some of devils, and some of angels, and thou hast to find out which of these attributes are accidental and which essential. Till thou knowest this, thou canst not find out where thy real happiness lies. The occupation of animals is eating, sleeping, and fighting; therefore, if thou art an animal, busy thyself in these things. Devils are busy in stirring up mischief, and in guile and deceit; if thou belongest to them, do their work. Angels contemplate the beauty of God, and are entirely free from animal qualities; if thou art of angelic nature, then strive towards thine origin, that thou mayest know and contemplate the Most High, and be delivered from the thralldom of lust and anger. Thou shouldest also discover why thou hast been created with these two animal instincts: whether that they should subdue and lead thee captive, or whether that thou shouldest subdue them, and, in thy upward progress, make of one thy steed and of the other thy weapon.[3]

The first step to self-knowledge is to know that thou art composed of an outward shape, called the body, and an inward entity called the heart or soul. By "heart" I do not mean the piece of flesh situated in the left of our bodies, but that which uses all the other faculties as its instruments and servants. In truth it does not belong to the visible world, but to the invisible, and has come into this world as a traveller visits a foreign

[3] Ghazzâlî's explanation of the animal and angelic nature of human beings, and the consequent need to develop the angelic characteristics, greatly influenced, among others, St. Thomas Aquinas, who incorporated it into the *Summa Theologica*, sometimes following Ghazzâlî's text verbatim. See Margaret Smith, *Al-Ghazâlî the Mystic* (London, 1944), pp. 221-22.

country for the sake of merchandise, and it will presently return to its native land. It is the knowledge of this entity and its attributes which is the key to the knowledge of God.

Some idea of the reality of the heart, or spirit, may be obtained by a man closing his eyes and forgetting everything around except his individuality. He will thus also obtain a glimpse of the unending nature of that individuality. Too close inquiry, however, into the essence of spirit is forbidden by the Law. In the Koran it is written: "They will question thee concerning the spirit. Say, 'The Spirit comes by the command of my Lord.'"[4] Thus much is known of it that it is an indivisible essence belonging to the world of decrees, and that it is not from everlasting but created. An exact philosophical knowledge of the spirit is not a necessary preliminary to walking in the path of religion, but comes rather as the result of self-discipline and perseverance in that path, as it is said in the Koran: "Those who strive in Our way, verily We will guide them to the right paths."[5]

For the carrying on of this spiritual warfare by which the knowledge of oneself and of God is to be obtained, the body may be figured as a kingdom, the soul as its king, and the different senses and faculties as constituting an army. Reason may be called the vizier, or prime minister, passion the revenue-collector, and anger the police-officer. Under the guise of collecting revenue, passion is continually prone to

---

[4] Koran, 17:85. The usual interpretation of this verse, in a narrow sense, is that it was intended as guidance for Muḥammad in replying to criticism of his prophetic mission by Jews and skeptics. Cf. Qayyum, *Letters*, p. 108: "The eternal God is found at a point within ourselves, which as the mystics hold, is equally God's central reality and ours, where spirit meets spirit."

[5] Koran, 29:69. Throughout this section, which is much longer in the Persian text, Ghazzâlî makes frequent allusions to the concept of *jihâd*, "striving." It should be noted, however, that he interprets jihâd as "spiritual warfare" not "holy war" and his martial imagery is purely symbolic in intent.

plunder on its own account, while resentment is always inclined to harshness and extreme severity. Both of these, the revenue-collector and the police-officer, have to be kept in subordination to the king, but not killed or excelled, as they have their own proper functions to fulfill. But if passion and resentment master reason, the ruin of the soul infallibly ensues. A soul which allows its lower faculties to dominate the higher is as one who should hand over an angel to the power of a dog or a Muslim to the tyranny of an unbeliever. The cultivation of demonic, animal, or angelic qualities results in the production of corresponding characters, which in the Day of Judgment will be manifested in visible shapes, the sensual appearing as swine, the ferocious as dogs and wolves, and the pure as angels. The aim of moral discipline is to purify the heart from the rust of passion and resentment, till, like a clear mirror, it reflects the light of God.

Someone may here object, "But if man has been created with animal and demonic qualities as well as angelic, how are we to know that the latter constitute his real essence, while the former are merely accidental and transitory?" To this I answer that the essence of each creature is to be sought in that which is highest in it and peculiar to it. Thus the horse and the ass are both burden-bearing animals, but the superiority of the horse to the ass consists in its being adapted for use in battle. If it fails in this, it becomes degraded to the rank of burden-bearing animals. Similarly with man: the highest faculty in him is reason, which fits him for the contemplation of God. If this predominates in him, when he dies, he leaves behind him all tendencies to passion and resentment, and becomes capable of association with angels. As regards his mere animal qualities, man is inferior to many animals, but reason makes him superior to them as it is written in the Koran: "To man We have subjected all things in the earth."[6] But if his lower tendencies have triumphed, after death he will ever be looking towards the earth and longing for earthly delights. Now the rational soul in man abounds in marvels, both of knowledge and power. By means of it he masters arts and sciences, can pass in a flash from earth to heaven and back again, can map out the skies and measure the distances between the stars. By it also he can draw the fish from the sea and the birds from the air, and can subdue to his service animals like the elephant, the camel, and the horse. His five senses are like five doors opening on the external world; but, more wonderful than this, his heart has a window which opens on the unseen world of spirits. In the state of sleep, when the avenues of the senses are closed, this window is opened and man receives impressions from the unseen world and sometimes foreshadowings of the future. His heart is then like a mirror which reflects what is pictured in the Tablet of Fate.[7] But, even in sleep, thoughts of worldly things dull this mirror, so that the impression it receives are not clear. After death, however, such thoughts vanish and things are seen in their naked reality, and the saying in the Koran is fulfilled: "We have stripped the veil from off thee and thy sight today is keen."[8]

This opening of a window in the heart towards the unseen also takes place in conditions approaching those of prophetic inspiration, when intuitions spring up in the mind unconveyed through any sense-channel. The more a man purifies himself from fleshly lusts and concentrates his mind on God, the more conscious will he be of such intuitions. Those who are not conscious of them have no right to deny their reality.

---

6 Koran, 45:13.

7 This is Field's translation of the expression *lawḥ maḥfûẓ*; see below, n. 8.

8 Koran, 50:22; cf. above, Introduction, p. 4, n. 1.

Nor are such intuitions confined only to those of prophetic rank. Just as iron, by sufficient polishing can be made into a mirror, so any mind by due discipline can be rendered receptive of such impressions. It was at this truth the Prophet hinted when he said, "Every child is born with a predisposition towards Islam; then his parents make a Jew, or a Christian, or a star-worshiper of him."[9] Every human being has in the depths of his consciousness heard the question "Am I not your Lord?"[10] and answered "Yes" to it. But some hearts are like mirrors so befouled with rust and dirt that they give no clear reflections, while those of the Prophets and saints, though they are men "of like passions with us"[11] are extremely sensitive to all divine impressions.

Nor is it only by reason of knowledge acquired and intuitive that the soul of man holds the first rank among created things, but also by reason of power. Just as angels preside over the elements, so does the soul rule the members of the body. Those souls which attain a special degree of power not only rule their own body but those of others also. If they wish a sick man to recover, he recovers, or a person in health to fall ill he becomes ill, or if they will the presence of a person he comes to them. According as the effects produced by these powerful souls are good or bad they are termed miracles or sorceries. These souls differ from common folk in three ways: (1) What others only see in dreams they see in their waking moments. (2) While others' wills only affect their own bodies, these, by will-power,

---

[9] A very well-known *ḥadîth*, or saying attributed to the Prophet Muḥammad. It is found in virtually all of the authoritative ḥadîth collections, including those of Bukhârî, Muslim, Tirmidhî, etc. See A. J. Wensinck, *A Handbook of Early Muhammadan Tradition* (reprint; Leiden, 1960), p. 45.

[10] An allusion to Koran 7:172.

[11] An allusion to Koran 18:110. This is one of several verses which emphasize the completely human character of the Prophet Muḥammad (often contrasted to the way Christians regard Jesus as divine).

can move bodies extraneous to themselves. (3) The knowledge which others acquire by laborious learning comes to them by intuition.

These three, of course, are not the only marks which differentiate them from common people, but the only ones that come within our cognizance. Just as no one knows the real nature of God but God Himself, so no one knows the real nature of a prophet but a prophet. Nor is this to be wondered at, as in everyday matters we see that it is impossible to explain the charm of poetry to one whose ear is insusceptible of cadence and rhythm, or the glories of color to one who is stone-blind. Besides mere incapacity, there are other hindrances to the attainment of spiritual truth. One of these is externally acquired knowledge. To use a figure, the heart may be represented as a well, and the five senses as five streams which are continually conveying water to it. In order to find out the real contents of the heart these streams must be stopped for a time, at any rate, and the refuse they have brought with them must be cleared out of the well. In other words, if we are to arrive at pure spiritual truth, we must put away, for the time, knowledge which has been acquired by external processes and which too often hardens into dogmatic prejudice.

A mistake of an opposite kind is made by shallow people who, echoing some phrases which they have caught from Sufi teachers, go about decrying all knowledge.[12] This is as if a

---

[12] This section gives only a very abridged version of the Persian text. By "knowledge," Ghazzâlî is referring primarily to *ᶜilm* (formal religious knowledge). It is very typical of him to emphasize that just as the religious scholar should not deride the mystical experience of the Sufi, the true Sufi should not disparage religious scholarship. In other writings, such as the autobiographical *Deliverance from Error*, Ghazzâlî made similar observations about the sciences: "the man who is loyal to Islam but ignorant...thinks that religion must be defended by rejecting every science connected with the philosophers, and so rejects all their sciences and accuses them of ignorance....

person who was not an adept in alchemy were to go about saying, "Alchemy is better than gold," and were to refuse gold when it was offered to him. Alchemy is better than gold, but real alchemists are very rare, and so are real Sufis. He who has a mere smattering of Sufism is not superior to a learned man, any more than he who has tried a few experiments in alchemy has ground for despising a rich man.

Anyone who will look into the matter will see that happiness is necessarily linked with the knowledge of God. Each faculty of ours delights in that for which it was created: lust delights in accomplishing desire, anger in taking vengeance, the eye in seeing beautiful objects, and the ear in hearing harmonious sounds. The highest function of the soul of man is the perception of truth; in this accordingly it finds its special delight. Even in trifling matters, such as learning chess, this holds good, and the higher the subject-matter of the knowledge obtained, the greater the delight. A man would be pleased at being admitted into the confidence of a prime minister, but how much more if the king makes an intimate of him and discloses state secrets to him!

An astronomer who, by his knowledge, can map the stars and describe their courses, derives more pleasure from his knowledge than the chess-player from his. Seeing, then, that nothing is higher than God, how great must be the delight which springs from the true knowledge of Him!

A person in whom the desire for this knowledge has disappeared is like one who has lost his appetite for healthy food, or who prefers feeding on clay to eating bread. All bodily appetites perish at death with the organs they use, but the soul

---

A grievous crime indeed against religion has been committed by the man who imagines that Islam is defended by the denial of the mathematical sciences...." (W. M. Watt, *The Faith and Practice of al-Ghazâlî*, p. 34.)

dies not, and retains whatever knowledge of God it possesses; nay, increases it.

An important part of our knowledge of God arises from the study and contemplation of our own bodies, which reveal to us the power, wisdom, and love of the Creator. His power, in that from a mere drop He has built up the wonderful frame of man; His wisdom is revealed in its intricacies and the mutual adaptability of its parts; and His love is shown by His not only supplying such organs as are absolutely necessary for existence, as the liver, the heart, and the brain, but those which are not absolutely necessary, as the hand, the foot, the tongue, and the eye. To these He has added, as ornaments, the blackness of the hair, the redness of lips, and the curve of the eyebrows.

Man has been truly termed a "microcosm," or little world in himself, and the structures of his body should be studied not only by those who wish to become doctors, but by those who wish to attain to a more intimate knowledge of God,[13] just as close study of the niceties and shades of language in a great poem reveals to us more and more of the genius of its author.

But, when all is said, the knowledge of the soul plays a more important part in leading to the knowledge of God than the knowledge of our body and the functions. The body may be compared to a steed and the soul to its rider; the body was created for the soul, the soul for the body. If a man knows not his own soul, which is the nearest thing to him, what is the use of his claiming to know others? It is as if a beggar who has not the wherewithal for a meal should claim to be able to feed a town.

In this chapter we have attempted in some degree to expound the greatness of man's soul. He who neglects it and suffers its capacities to rust or to degenerate must necessarily

---

[13] On this idea, see above, n. 2.

be the loser in this world and the next. The true greatness of man lies in his capacity for eternal progress, otherwise in this temporal sphere he is the weakest of all things, being subject to hunger, thirst, heat, cold, and sorrow. Those things he takes most delight in are often the most injurious to him, and those things which benefit him are not to be obtained without toil and trouble. As to his intellect, a slight disarrangement of matter in his brain is sufficient to destroy or madden him; as to his power, the sting of a wasp is sufficient to rob him of ease of sleep; as to his temper, he is upset by the loss of a sixpence; as to his beauty, he is little more than nauseous matter covered with a fair skin. Without frequent washing he becomes utterly repulsive and disgraceful.

In truth, man in this world is extremely weak and contemptible; it is only in the next that he will be of value, if by means of the "alchemy of happiness" he rises from the rank of beasts to that of angels. Otherwise his condition will be worse than the brutes, which perish and turn to dust. It is necessary for him, at the same time that he is conscious of his superiority as the climax of created things, to learn to know also his helplessness, as that too is one of the keys to the knowledge of God.

Chapter Two
Knowledge of God

It is a well-known saying of the Prophet that "He who knows himself, knows God"; that is, by contemplation of his own being and attributes man arrives at some knowledge of God. But since many who contemplate themselves do not find God, it follows that there must be some special way of doing so. As a matter of fact, there are two methods of arriving at this knowledge, but one is so abstruse that it is not adapted to ordinary intelligences, and therefore is better left unexplained. The other method is as follows. When a man considers himself he knows that there was a time when he was non-existent, as it is written in the Koran: "Does it not occur to man that there was a time when he was nothing?"[1] Further, he knows that he was made out of a drop of water in which there was neither intellect, nor hearing, sight, head, hands, feet, etc. From this it is obvious that, whatever degree of perfection he may have arrived at, he did not make himself, nor can he now make a single hair.

How much more helpless, then, was his condition when he was a mere drop of water! Thus, as we have seen in the first chapter, he finds in his own being reflected in miniature, so to speak, the power, wisdom, and love of the Creator. If all the sages of the world were assembled, and their lives prolonged for an indefinite time, they could not effect any improvement in the construction of a single part of the body.

---

[1] A free translation of Koran 76:1.

For instance, in the adaptation of the front and side-teeth to the mastication of food, and in the construction of the tongue, salivating glands, and throat for its deglutition, we find a contrivance which cannot be improved upon. Similarly, whoever considers his hand, with its five fingers of unequal lengths, four of them with three joints and the thumb with only two, and the way in which it can be used for grasping, or for carrying, or for smiting, will frankly acknowledge that no amount of human wisdom could better it by altering the number and arrangement of the fingers, or in any other way.

When a man further considers how his various wants of food, lodging, etc., are amply supplied from the storehouse of creation, he becomes aware that God's mercy is as great as His power and wisdom, as He has Himself said, "My mercy is greater than My wrath,"[2] and according to the Prophet's saying, "God is more tender to His servants than a mother to her suckling-child."[3] Thus from his own creation man comes to know God's existence, from the wonders of his bodily frame God's power and wisdom, and from the ample provision made for his various needs God's love. In this way the knowledge of oneself becomes a key to the knowledge of God.

---

[2] Attributing a quotation to God usually implies the citation of a Koranic verse. In this case, however, Ghazzâlî is referring not to the Koran but to a well-known *ḥadîth qudsî*—a divinely inspired utterance by the Prophet Muḥammad quoting God as saying something but one which is not regarded as part of the revelation that makes up the Koran. The ḥadîth qudsî thus combines features of both conventional ḥadith (reports of things the Prophet Muḥammad said on his own authority) and the Koran (direct revelation from God); on this phenomenon, see William Graham, *Divine Word and Prophetic Word in Early Islam* (The Hague, 1977). This particular tradition is described by Graham, *Prophetic Word*, pp. 184-85 (#59).

[3] A fairly well-known *ḥadîth* cited by al-Bukhârî, *Ṣaḥîḥ* (Leiden, 1862-1908), 78/18; Ibn Mâja, *Sunan* (Cairo, 1313/1895-96), 37/35.

Not only are man's attributes a reflection of God's attributes, but the mode of existence of man's soul affords some insight into God's mode of existence. That is to say, both God and the soul are invisible, indivisible, unconfined by space and time, and outside the categories of quantity and quality; nor can the ideas of shape, color, or size attach to them. People find it hard to form a conception of such realities as are devoid of quality and quantity, etc., but a similar difficulty attaches to the conception of our everyday feeling, such as anger, pain, pleasure, or love. They are thought-concepts and cannot be cognized by the senses; whereas quality, quantity, etc. are sense-concepts. Just as the ear cannot take cognizance of color, nor the eye of sound, so, in conceiving of the ultimate realities, God and the soul, we find ourselves in a region in which sense-concepts can bear no part. So much, however, we can see, that, as God is Ruler of the universe, and being Himself beyond space and time, quantity and quality, [He] governs things that are so conditioned, so that soul rules the body and its members, being itself invisible, indivisible, and unlocated in any special part. For how can the indivisible be located in that which is divisible? From all this we see how true is the saying of the Prophet, "God created man in His own likeness."[4]

And, as we arrive at some knowledge of God's essence and attributes from the contemplation of the soul's essence and attributes, so we come to understand God's method of working

[4] Bukhârî, *Ṣaḥîḥ*, 79/1; Muslim, *Ṣaḥîḥ* (Cairo, 1283/1866-67), 45/115. Strictly speaking, the ḥadîth says that God created *Adam* in his own image, but this is understood as applying to all mankind. In terms of the history of Muslim theology, this concept was potentially dangerous since it implied an element of *tashbîh*, or anthropomorphism. Ghazzâlî, however, makes it clear that "image" does not mean physical form; see above, Chapter One, n. 2. This ḥadîth seems to have been one of Ghazzâlî's favorites; it also figures in his *Jawâhir al-qur'ân,* translated by M. A. Quasem, *The Jewels of the Qur'ân* (London, 1983), p. 51.

and government and delegation of power to angelic forces, etc., by observing how each of us governs his own little kingdom. To take a simple instance: suppose a man wishes to write the name of God.[5] First of all the wish is conceived in his heart, it is then conveyed to the brain by the vital spirits, the form of the word "God" takes shape in the thought-chambers of the brain, thence it travels by the nerve channels, and sets in motion the fingers, which in their turn set in motion the pen, and thus the name "God" is traced on paper exactly as it had been conceived in the writer's brain. Similarly, when God wills a thing it appears in the spiritual plane, which in the Koran is called "The Throne;"[6] from the throne it passes, by a spiritual current, to a lower plane called "The Chair;"[7] then the shape of

---

[5] Literally, the *b'ismillâh* ("in the name of God"), a conventional formula used at the beginning of all writings, formal speeches, etc.

[6] In the Persian text, Ghazzâlî specifically cites Koran 10:3—"[God] is firmly established on the Throne, regulating and governing all things." This is one of several places where the Koran (7:52; 13:2; etc.) speaks of God being "firmly established on the throne (*ᶜarsh*)." Despite the anthropomorphist implications of the idea of God "sitting" on a throne, many Muslims insisted on a literalist interpretation of this and other verses. The dominant Ashᶜârî theology of Sunni Islam rejected anthropomorphism, but insisted on acceptance of such verses as an article of faith, "without asking how." In Ghazzâlî's interpretation here, which is highly reminiscent of the Neo-Platonic theory of "emanations," he is clearly favoring an allegorical interpretation to distance himself from charges of *tashbîh*.

[7] Known as *al-kursî*. This term occurs in this sense only in the famous "Throne Verse" of the Koran (2:255); the other occurrence of the word refers to the throne of Solomon. Theologians and exegetes of the Koran were somewhat puzzled by the use of this term along with *ᶜarsh* (see the preceding note): What is the difference between God's "throne" (*ᶜarsh*) and His "chair" (*kursî*)? Were the two terms simply synonyms or fundamentally different? How could a non-anthropomorphic God "sit" on a throne or chair? Should these words be explained literally or symbolically? On this important issue, see the article "Kursî" in the *Encyclopaedia of Islam* (new edition; Leiden, in progress), 5:509 (hereafter cited as EI_2).

it appears on the "Tablet of Destiny;"[8] whence, by the mediation of the forces called "angels" it assumes actuality, and appears on the earth in the form of plants, trees, and animals, representing the will and thought of God, as the written letters represent the wish conceived in the heart and the shape present in the brain of the writer.

No one can understand a king but a king; therefore God has made each of us a king in miniature, so to speak, over a kingdom which is an infinitely reduced copy of His own. In the kingdom of man God's "throne" is represented by the soul; the Archangel by the heart, "the chair" by the brain, "the tablet" by the treasure chamber of thought. The soul, itself unlocated and indivisible, governs the body as God governs the universe. In short, each of us is entrusted with a little kingdom, and charged not to be careless in the administration of it.

As regards the recognition of God's providence, there are many degrees of Knowledge. The mere physicist is like an ant who, crawling on a sheet of paper and observing black letters spreading over it, should refer the cause to the pen alone. The astronomer is like an ant of somewhat wider vision who should catch sight of the fingers moving the pen, i.e., he knows that the elements are under the power of the stars, but he does not know that the stars are under the power of the angels. Thus, owing to the different degrees of perception in people, disputes

---

[8] This term, properly transliterated as *al-lawḥ al-maḥfûẓ*, comes from the Koran, 85:22, where it seems to refer to the Koran itself. Literalist theologians interpreted this to mean the original copy of the Koran preserved on tablets in heaven (cf. Ghazzâlî, *Pearl*, p. 63); others took it in a rather predestinarian sense to mean the records of all the actions that have been or will be taken on earth; mystics and philosophers interpreted it in various allegorical ways. Here, Ghazzâlî attaches his own highly technical meaning to the term, which serves as a powerful image throughout his writings: see Hazarvi, *Mysteries of the Human Soul*, pp. 36-47; A. J. Wensinck, *On the Relation between Ghazâlî's Cosmology and his Mysticism* (Amsterdam, 1933).

must arise in tracing effects to causes. Those whose eyes never see beyond the world of phenomena are like those who mistake servants of the lowest rank for the king. The laws of phenomena must be constant, or there could be no such thing as science; but it is a great error to mistake the slaves for the master.

As long as this difference in the perceptive faculty of observers exists, disputes must necessarily go on. It is as if some blind men, hearing that an elephant had come to their town, should go and examine it. The only knowledge of it which they can obtain comes through the sense of touch; so one handles the animal's leg, another his tusk, another his ear, and, according to their several perceptions, pronounce it to be a column, a thick pole, or a quilt, each taking a part for the whole.[9] So the physicist and astronomer confound the laws they perceive with the Lawgiver. A similar mistake is attributed to Abraham in the Koran, where it is related that he turned successively to stars, moon, and sun as the objects of his worship, till grown aware of Him who had made all these, he exclaimed, "I love not them that set."[10]

We have a common instance of this referring to second causes what ought to be referred to the First Cause in the case

---

[9] Most English readers will be familiar with this popular story. It is probably of Indian origin but was well known in the Muslim world; it also appears in Rûmî's great mystical poem, the *Mathnawî*: See R. A. Nicholson, *The Mathnawî of Jalâlu'ddin Rûmî* (London, 1930; reprint, 1977), 2:71.

[10] Koran, 6:76. In the *Mi*ᶜ*yâr al-*ᶜ*ilm*, Ghazzâlî made use of this idea of those who "love not them that set" to refer to the "elect of the elect;" see Smith, *Ghazâlî*, p. 34. Some Muslims would dispute Ghazzâlî's suggestion that Abraham practiced an astral religion. According to the modern Muslim interpreter of the Koran, ᶜAbd Allah Yûsuf ᶜAlî, *Tarjama ma*ᶜ*ânî al-qur'ân al-karîm* (Riyadh, n.d.), p. 309 n. 898, "This allegory shows the stages of Abraham's spiritual development. It should not be supposed that he literally worshipped stars or heavenly bodies."

of so-called illness. For instance, if a man ceases to take any interest in worldly matters, conceives a distaste for common pleasures, and appears sunk in depression, the doctor will say, "This is a case of melancholy, and requires such and such a prescription." The physicist will say, "This is a dryness of the brain caused by hot weather and cannot be relieved till the air becomes moist." The astrologer will attribute it to some particular conjunction or opposition of the planets. "Thus far their wisdom reaches," says the Koran.[11] It does not occur to them that what has really happened is this: that the Almighty has a concern for the welfare of that man, and has therefore commanded His servants, the planets or the elements, to produce such a condition in him that he may turn away from the world to his Maker. The knowledge of this fact is a lustrous pearl from the ocean of inspirational knowledge, to which all other forms of knowledge are as islands in the sea.

The doctor, physicist, and astrologer are doubtless right each in his particular branch of knowledge, but they do not see that illness is, so to speak, a cord of love by which God draws to Himself the saints concerning whom He has said, "I was sick and ye visited Me not."[12] Illness itself is one of those forms of experience by which man arrives at the knowledge of God, as he says by the mouth of His prophet, "Sicknesses themselves are My servants, and are attached to My chosen."[13]

---

[11] Koran, 53:30.

[12] This is another example of a *ḥadîth qudsî* (above, n. 2). Many of these special traditions are similar to passages from non-Muslim scripture, and the parallel of this quotation to Christ's parable of the Last Judgment (Matthew 24:41-45) has been noted by Smith, *Ghazâlî*, p. 117 and Graham, *Divine Word*, pp. 179-80; see also EI_2, 3:28-29. Ghazzâlî repeats this same saying in a fuller form later in this work; see below, Chapter Eight, n. 7.

[13] This would appear to be another *ḥadîth qudsî*, but I have not been able to identify it. It also does not appear in the Persian text.

The foregoing remarks may enable us to enter a little more fully into the meaning of those exclamations so often on the lips of the Faithful: "God is holy," "Praise be to God," "There is no god but God," "God is great." Concerning the last we may say that it does not mean that God is greater than creation, for creation is His manifestation as light manifests the sun, and it would not be correct to say that the sun is greater than its own light. It rather means that God's greatness immeasurably transcends our cognitive faculties, and that we can only form a very dim and imperfect idea of it. If a child asks us to explain to him the pleasure which exists in wielding sovereignty, we may say it is like the pleasure he feels in playing bat and ball, though in reality the two have nothing in common except that they both come under the category of pleasure.

Thus, the exclamation, "God is great" means that His greatness far exceeds all our powers of comprehension. Moreover, such imperfect knowledge of God as we can attain to is not a mere speculative knowledge, but must be accompanied by devotion and worship. When a man dies he has to do with God alone, and if we have to live with a person, our happiness entirely depends on the degree of affection we feel towards him. Love is the seed of happiness, and love of God is fostered and developed by worship.

Such worship and constant remembrance of God implies a certain degree of austerity and curbing of bodily appetites. Not that a man is intended altogether to abolish these, for then the human race would perish. But strict limits must be set to their indulgence, and as a man is not the best judge in his own case as to what these limits should be, he had better consult some spiritual guide on the subject. Such spiritual guides are the prophets, and the laws which they have laid down under divine inspiration prescribe the limits which must be observed in these matters. "He who transgresses these limits wrongs his own soul," as it is written in the Koran.[14]

Notwithstanding this clear pronouncement of the Koran there are those who, through their ignorance of God, do transgress these limits, and this ignorance may be due to several different causes: Firstly, there are some who, failing to find God by observation, conclude that there is no God and that this world of wonders made itself, or existed from everlasting. They are like a man who, seeing a beautifully written letter, should suppose that it had written itself without a writer, or had always existed. People in this state of mind are so far gone in error that it is of little use to argue with them. Such are some of the physicists and astronomers to whom we referred above.

Some, through ignorance of the real nature of the soul, repudiate the doctrine of a future life, in which man will be called to account and be rewarded or punished. They regard themselves as no better than animals or vegetables, and equally perishable. Some, on the other hand, believe in God and a future life but with a weak belief. They say to themselves, "God is great and independent of us; our worship or abstinence from worship is a matter of entire indifference to Him." Their state of mind is like that of a sick man who, when prescribed a certain regime by his doctor, should say, "Well, if I follow it or don't follow it, what does it matter to the doctor?" It certainly does not matter to the doctor, but the patient may destroy himself by his disobedience. Just as surely as unchecked sickness of body ends in bodily death, so does uncured disease of the soul end in future misery, according to the saying of the

---

[14] Koran, 65:1. This verse discusses the subject of divorce and then states, "Those are limits set by God: and any who transgresses the limits of God, does verily wrong his (own) soul."

Koran, "Only those shall be saved who come to God with a sound heart."[15]

A fourth kind of unbelievers are those who say, "The Law tells us to abstain from anger, lust, and hypocrisy. This is plainly impossible, for man is created with these qualities inherent in him. You might as well tell us to make black white." Those foolish people ignore the fact that the law does not tell us to uproot these passions, but to restrain them within due limits, so that, by avoiding the great sins, we may obtain forgiveness of the smaller ones. Even the Prophet of God said, "I am a man like you, and get angry like others;" and in the Koran it is written, "God loves those who swallow down their anger,"[16] not those who have no anger at all.

A fifth class lay stress on the beneficence of God, and ignore His justice, saying to themselves, "Well, whatever we do, God is merciful." They do not consider that, though God is merciful, thousands of human beings perish miserably in hunger and disease. They know that whosoever wishes for a livelihood, or for wealth, or learning, must not merely say, "God is merciful," but must exert himself. Although the Koran says, "Every living creature's support comes from God," it is also written, "Man obtains nothing except by striving."[17] The fact is, such teaching is really from the devil, and such people only speak with their lips and not with their heart.

A sixth class claim to have reached such a degree of sanctity that sin cannot affect them. Yet, it you treat one of them with disrespect, he will bear a grudge against you for years, and if one of them be deprived of a morsel of food which he thinks his due, the whole world will appear dark and narrow

[15] Koran, 26:89, referring to Judgment Day.

[16] Koran, 3:134.

[17] Koran 11:6 and 53:39. These verses figured prominently in the debate over predestination in Islamic theology.

to him. Even if any of them do really conquer their passions, they have no right to make such a claim, for the prophets, the highest of human kind, constantly confessed and bewailed their sins. Some of them had such a dread of sin that they even abstained from lawful things; thus it is related of the Prophet that, one day, when a date had been brought to him he would not eat it, as he was not sure that it had been lawfully obtained. Whereas these free-lives will swallow gallons[18] of wine and claim (I shudder as I write) to be superior to the Prophet whose sanctity was endangered by a date, while theirs is unaffected by all that wine! Surely they deserve that the devil should drag them down to perdition. Real saints know that he who does not master his appetites does not deserve the name of a man, and the true Muslim is one who will cheerfully acknowledge the limits imposed by the Law. He who endeavors, on whatever pretext, to ignore its obligations is certainly under Satanic influence, and should be talked to, not with a pen but with a sword. These pseudo mystics sometimes pretend to be drowned in a sea of wonder, but if you ask them what they are wondering at they do not know. They should be told to wonder as much as they please, but at the same time to remember that the Almighty is their Creator and that they are His servants.

---

[18] Literally *qadaḥ-hâ*, cups or bowls.

The Mystic Dance of Ecstasy. The Sufi Muḥammad Tabâdkânî (d. 1486) is shown dancing while his followers play musical intruments. Normally regarded as unlawful by Muslim pietists, Ghazzâlî regarded this as an acceptable mystical practice (as discussed in Chapter Six). From a manuscript of Kâzargâhî's *Majâlis al-ʿUshshâq* (*Assemblies of the Lovers [of God]*) in the Bodleian Library, Ouseley Add. 24, f. 191r. (Reproduced by permission of the Bodleian Library, Oxford)

Chapter Three
Knowledge of This World

This world is a stage or market-place passed by pilgrims on their way to the next. It is here that they provide themselves with provisions for the way; or, to put it plainly, man acquires here, by the use of his bodily senses, some knowledge of the works of God, and, through them, of God Himself, the sight of whom will constitute his future beatitude. It is for the acquirement of this knowledge that the spirit of man has descended into this world of water and clay. As long as his senses remain with him he is said to be "in this world;" when they depart, and only his essential attributes remain, he is said to have gone to "the next world."

While man is in this world, two things are necessary for him: first, the protection and nurture of his soul; secondly, the care and nurture of his body. The proper nourishment of the soul, as above shown, is the knowledge and love of God, and to be absorbed in the love of anything but God is the ruin of the soul. The body, so to speak, is simply the riding-animal of the soul and perishes while the soul endures. The soul should take care of the body, just as a pilgrim on his way to Mecca takes care of his camel; but if the pilgrim spends his whole time in feeding and adorning his camel, the caravan will leave him behind, and he will perish in the desert.

Man's bodily needs are simple, being comprised under three heads: food, clothing, and a dwelling-place; but the bodily desires which were implanted in him with a view to procuring these are apt to rebel against reason, which is of later growth than they. Accordingly, as we saw above, they require to be curbed and restrained by the divine laws promulgated by the prophets.

Considering the world with which we have for a time to do, we find it divided into three departments—animal, vegetable, and mineral. The products of all three are continually needed by man and have given rise to three principal occupations—those of the weaver, the builder, and the worker in metal. These, again, have many subordinate branches, such as tailors, masons, smiths, etc. None can be quite independent of others; this gives rise to various business-connections and relations and those too frequently afford occasions for hatred, envy, jealousy, and other maladies of the soul. Hence come quarrels and strife, and the need of political and civil government and knowledge of law.

Thus the occupations and businesses of the world have become more and more complicated and troublesome, chiefly owing to the fact that men have forgotten that their real necessities are only three—clothing, food, and shelter, and that these exist only with the object of making the body a fit vehicle for the soul in its journey towards the next world. They have fallen into the same mistake as the pilgrim to Mecca, mentioned above, who, forgetting the object of his pilgrimage and himself, should spend his whole time in feeding and adorning his camel. Unless a man maintains the strictest watch he is certain to be fascinated and entangled by the world, which, as the Prophet said, is "a more potent sorcerer than Harut and Marut."[1]

---

[1] The Koran, 2:102, says: "...the blasphemers were not Solomon but the evil ones, teaching men magic, and such things as came down at Babylon to the angels Hârût and Mârût." The identity of these two angels, and the question of what exactly they taught, has been an object of considerable speculation by commentators on the Koran.

The deceitful character of the world comes out in the following ways. In the first place, it pretends that it will always remain with you, while, as a matter of fact, it is slipping away from you, moment by moment, and bidding you farewell, like a shadow which seems stationary, but is actually always moving. Again, the world presents itself under the guise of a radiant but immoral sorceress, pretends to be in love with you, fondles you, and then goes off to your enemies, leaving you to die of chagrin and despair. Jesus (upon whom be peace!) saw the world revealed in the form of an ugly old hag. He asked her how many husbands she had possessed; she replied that they were countless. He asked whether they had died or been divorced; she said that she had slain them all. "I marvel," he said, "at the fools who see what you have done to others, and still desire you."

This sorceress decks herself out in gorgeous and jewelled apparel and veils her face. Then she goes forth to seduce men, too many of whom follow her to their own destruction. The Prophet has said that on the Judgment Day the world will appear in the form of a hideous witch with green eyes and projecting teeth. Man, beholding her, will say, "Mercy on us! who is this?" The angels will answer, "This is the world for whose sake you quarreled and fought and embittered one another's lives." Then she will be cast into hell, whence she will cry out, "O Lord! where are those, my former lovers?" God will then command that they be cast after her.

Whoever will seriously contemplate the past eternity during which the world was not in existence, and the future eternity during which it will not be in existence, will see that it is essentially like a journey, in which the stages are represented by years, the leagues by months, the miles by days, and the steps by moments. What words, then, can picture the folly of the man who endeavors to make it his permanent abode, and forms plans ten years ahead regarding things he may never need, seeing that very possibly he may be under the ground in ten days!

Those who have indulged without limit in the pleasures of the world, at the time of death will be like a man who has gorged himself to repletion on delicious viands and then vomits them up. The deliciousness has gone, but the disgrace remains. The greater the abundance of the possession which they have enjoyed in the shape of gardens, male and female slaves, gold, silver, etc., the more keenly they well feel the bitterness of parting from them. This is a bitterness which will outlast death, for the soul which has contracted covetousness as a fixed habit will necessarily in the next world suffer from the pangs of unsatisfied desire.

Another dangerous property of worldly things is that they at first appear as mere trifles, but each of these so-called "trifles" branches out into countless ramification until they swallow up the whole of a man's time and energy. Jesus (on whom be peace!) said, "The lover of the world is like a man drinking sea-water; the more he drinks, the more thirsty he gets, till at last he perishes with thirst unquenched." The Prophet said, "You can no more mix with the world without being contaminated by it than you can go into water without getting wet."

The world is like a table spread for successive relays of guests who come and go. There are gold and silver dishes, abundance of food and perfumes. The wise guest eats as much as is sufficient for him, smells the perfumes, thanks his host, and departs. The foolish guest, on the other hand, tries to carry off some of the gold and silver dishes, only to find them wrenched out of his hands and himself thrust forth, disappointed and disgraced.

We may close these illustrations of the deceitfulness of the world with the following short parable. Suppose a ship to arrive at a certain well-wooded island. The captain of the ship tells the passengers he will stop a few hours there, but warns them not to delay too long. Accordingly the passengers disembark and stroll in different directions. The wisest, however, return after a short time, and, finding the ship empty, choose the most comfortable place in it. A second band of the passengers spend a somewhat longer time on the island, admiring the foliage of the trees and listening to the song of the birds. Coming on board, they find the best places in the ship already occupied, and have to content themselves with the less comfortable ones. A third party wander still farther, and, finding some brilliantly colored stones, carry them back to the ship. Their lateness in coming on board compels them to stow themselves away in the lower part of the ship, where they find their loads of stones, which by this time have lost all their brilliancy, very much in their way. The last group go so far in their wanderings that they get quite out of reach of the captain's voice calling them to come on board, and at last he has to sail away without them. They wander about in a hopeless condition and finally either perish of hunger or fall a prey to wild beasts.

The first group represents the faithful who keep aloof from the world altogether and the last group the infidels who care only for this world and nothing for the next.[2] The two intermediate classes are those who preserve their faith, but entangle themselves more or less with the vanities of things present.

Although we have said so much against the world, it must be remembered that there are some things in the world which are not *of* it, such as knowledge and good deeds. A man carries

---

[2] Cf. Koran 16:107—"They love the life of this world better than the hereafter...."

what knowledge he possesses with him into the next world, and though his good deeds have passed, yet the effect of them remains in his character. Especially is this the case with acts of devotion, which result in the perpetual remembrance and love of God. These are among "those good things" which, as the Koran says, "pass not away."[3]

Other good things there are in the world, such as marriage, food, clothing, etc., which a wise man uses just in proportion as they help him to attain to the next world. Other things which engross the mind, causing it to cleave to this world and to be careless of the next, are purely evil and were alluded to by the Prophet when he said, "The world is a curse, and all which is in it is a curse, except the remembrance of God, and that which aids it."

---

[3] Koran, 19:76: "...the good things that endure, good deeds, are best in the sight of thy Lord...."

Chapter Four
Knowledge of the Next World

As regards the joys of heaven and the pains of hell which will follow this life, all believers in the Koran and the Traditions are sufficiently informed. But it often escapes them that there is also a spiritual heaven and hell, concerning the former of which God said to His Prophet, "Eye hath not seen, nor ear heard, neither hath it entered into the heart of man to conceive the things which are prepared for the righteous."[1] In the heart of the enlightened man there is a window opening on the realities of the spiritual world, so that he knows, not by hearsay or traditional belief, but by actual experience, what produces wretchedness or happiness in the soul just as clearly and decidedly as the Physician knows what produces sickness or health in the body. He recognizes that knowledge of God and worship are medicinal, and that ignorance and sin are deadly poisons for the soul. Even many so-called "learned" men, from blindly following others' opinions, have no real certainty in their beliefs regarding the happiness or misery of souls in the next world, but he who will attend to the matter with a mind unbiased by prejudice will arrive at clear convictions on this matter.

The effect of death on the composite nature of man is as follows: Man has two souls, an animal soul and a spiritual soul, which latter is of angelic nature. The seat of the animal soul is

---

1 Another *ḥadîth qudsî*. See Graham, *Divine Word*, pp. 117-19 (#2).

the heart, from which this soul issues like a subtle vapor and pervades all the members of the body, giving the power of sight to the eye, the power of hearing to the ear, and to every member the faculty of performing its own appropriate functions. It may be compared to a lamp carried about within a cottage, the light of which falls upon the walls wherever it goes. The heart is the wick of this lamp, and when the supply of oil is cut off for any reason, the lamp dies. Such is the death of the animal soul. With the spiritual, or human soul, the case is different. It is indivisible, and by it man knows God. It is, so to speak, the rider of the animal soul, and when that perishes it still remains, but is like a horseman who has been dismounted, or like a hunter who has lost his weapons. That steed and those weapons were granted the human soul that by means of them it might pursue and capture the Phoenix[2] of the love and knowledge of God. If it *has* effected that capture, it is not a grief but rather a relief to be able to lay those weapons aside, and to dismount from that weary steed. Therefore the Prophet said, "Death is a welcome gift of God to the believer." But alas for that soul which loses its steed and hunting weapons before it has captured the prize! Its misery and regret will be indescribable.

A little further consideration will show how entirely distinct the human soul is from the body and its members. Limb after limb may be paralyzed and cease working, but the individuality of the soul is unimpaired. Further, the body which you have now is no longer the body which you had as a child, but entirely different, yet your personality now is identical with your personality then. It is therefore easy to conceive of it as

[2] The Persian text does not use this metaphor. It was perhaps added by a subsequent editor as the use of the phoenix as a symbol of mystical knowledge was common in later Persian poetry (notably in Farîd al-Dîn ᶜAṭṭâr's *Manṭiq al-ṭayr* or *Language of the Birds*).

persisting when the body is done with altogether, along with its essential attributes which were independent of the body, such as the knowledge and love of God. This is the meaning of the saying, "The good things abide."[3] But if, instead of carrying away with you knowledge, you depart in ignorance of God, this ignorance also is an essential attribute, and will abide as darkness of soul and the seed of misery. Therefore the Koran says, "He who is blind in this life will be blind in the next life and astray from the path."[4]

The reason of the human spirit seeking to return to that upper world is that its origin was from thence, and that it is of angelic nature. It was sent down into this lower sphere against its will to acquire knowledge and experience, as God said in the Koran: "Go down from hence, all of you; there will come to you instruction from Me, and they who obey the instruction need not fear, neither shall they be grieved."[5] The verse, "I breathed into man of My spirit,"[6] also points to the celestial origin of the human soul. Just as the health of the animal soul consists in the equilibrium of its component parts, and this equilibrium is restored, when impaired, by appropriate medicine, so the health of the human soul consists in a moral equilibrium which is maintained and repaired, when needful, by ethical instruction and moral precepts.

As regards its future existence, we have already seen that the human soul is essentially independent of the body. All objections to its existence after death based on the supposed necessity of its recovering its former body fall, therefore, to the ground. Some theologians have supposed that the human soul is annihilated after death and then restored, but this is contrary

---

3 A phrase taken from the Koran, 16:107; cf. above, Chapter Three, n. 3.

4 Koran, 17:72.

5 Koran, 2:36.

6 Based on Koran, 15:29 and 38:71-72.

both to reason and to the Koran.[7] The former shows us that death does not destroy the essential individuality of a man, and the Koran says, "Think not that those who are slain in the path of God are dead; nay, they are alive, rejoicing in the presence of their Lord, and in the grace bestowed on them."[8] Not a word is said in the Law about any of the dead, good or bad, being annihilated. Nay, the Prophet is said to have questioned the spirits of slain infidels as to whether they had found the punishments with which he had threatened them real or not. When his followers asked him what was the good of questioning them, he replied, "They hear my words better than you do."

Some Sufis have had the unseen world of heaven and hell revealed to them when in a state of death-like trance. On their recovering consciousness their faces betray the nature of the revelations they have had by marks of joy or terror. But no visions are necessary to prove what will occur to every thinking man, that when death has stripped him of his senses and left him nothing but his bare personality, if while on earth he has too closely attached himself to objects perceived by the senses, such as wives, children, wealth, lands, slaves, male and female, etc., he must necessarily suffer when bereft of those objects. Whereas, on the contrary, if he has as far as possible turned his back on all earthly objects and fixed his supreme affection upon God, he will welcome death as a means of escape from

---

[7] The question of what happened to the soul in the interval between death and resurrection was hotly debated, especially since the notion that the soul lingered around the tomb in a more or less conscious, or even active, state supported the rituals of visiting and venerating the tombs of saints. Sufis like Ghazzâlî supported this popular practice but conservative religious leaders regarded it as an unacceptable innovation. A good introduction to this subject may be found in Jane Smith and Yvonne Haddad, *The Islamic Understanding of Death and Resurrection* (Albany, 1981), pp. 31-61.

[8] Koran, 3:169.

worldly entanglements, and of union with Him whom he loves. In his case, the Prophet's sayings will be verified: "Death is a bridge which unites friend to friend," and "The world is a paradise for infidels, but a prison for the faithful."[9]

On the other hand, the pains which souls suffer after death all have their source in excessive love of the world. The Prophet said that every unbeliever, after death, will be tormented by ninety-nine snakes, each having nine heads. Some simple-minded people have examined the graves of unbelievers and wondered at failing to see these snakes. They do not understand that these snakes have their abode within the unbeliever's spirit, and they existed in him even before he died, for they were his own evil qualities symbolized, such as jealousy, hatred, hypocrisy, pride, deceit, etc., every one of which springs, directly or remotely, from love of the world. Such is the doom of those who, in the words of the Koran, "set their hearts on this world rather than on the next."[10] If those snakes were merely external they might hope to escape their torment, if it were but for a moment; but being their own inherent attributes, how can they escape?

Take, for instance, the case of a man who has sold a slave-girl without knowing how much he was attached to her till she is quite out of his reach. Then the love of her, hitherto dormant, wakes up in him with such intensity as to amount to torture, stinging him like a snake, so that he would fain cast himself into fire or water to escape it. Such is the effect of love of the world, which those who have it often suspect not till the world is taken from them, and then the torment of vain longing is such that they would gladly exchange it for any number of mere external snakes and scorpions.

---

[9] A well-known *ḥadîth* cited by Muslim, *Ṣaḥîḥ*, 53/1; Tirmidhî, *Ṣaḥîḥ* (Cairo, 1292/1875-76), 34/16; Ibn Mâja, *Sunan*, 37/3.

[10] Koran, 16:107.

Every sinner thus carries with him into the world beyond death the instruments of his own punishment; and the Koran says truly, "Verily you shall see hell; you shall see it with the eye of certainty,"[11] and "hell surrounds the unbelievers."[12] It does not say "will surround them" for it is round them even now.

Some may object, "If such is the case, then who can escape hell, for who is not more or less bound to the world by various ties of affection and interest?" To this we answer that there are some, notably the fakirs,[13] who have entirely disengaged themselves from love of the world. But even among those who have worldly possessions such as wife, children, houses, etc., there are those who, though they have some affection for these, love God yet more. Their case is like that of a man who, though he may have a dwelling which he is fond of in one city, when he is called by the king to take up a post of authority in another city, does so gladly, as the post of authority is dearer to him than his former dwelling. Such are many of the prophets and saints.

Others there are, and a great number, who have some love to God but the love of the world so preponderates in them that they will have to suffer a good deal of pain after death before they are thoroughly weaned from it. Many profess to love God, but a man may easily test himself by watching which way the balance of his affection inclines when the commands of God come into collision with some of his desires. The profession of love to God which is insufficient to restrain from disobedience to God is a lie.

We have seen above that one kind of spiritual hell is the forcible separation from worldly things to which the heart

[11] Koran, 102:6-7.

[12] Koran, 9:49.

[13] The Persian text has dervish rather than fakir.

cleaves too fondly. Many carry about within them the germs of such a hell without being aware of it; hereafter they will be like some king who, after living in luxury, has been dethroned and made a laughing stock. The second kind of spiritual hell is that of shame, when a man wakes up to see the nature of the actions he committed in their naked reality. Thus he who slandered will see himself in the guise of a cannibal eating his dead brother's flesh, and he who envied as one who casts stones against a wall, which stones, rebounding, put out the eyes of his own children.

This species of hell, i. e., of shame, may be symbolized by the following short parable: Suppose a certain king has been celebrating his son's marriage. In the evening the young man goes off with some companions and presently returns to the palace (as he thinks) intoxicated. He enters a chamber where a light is burning and lies down, as he supposes by his bride. In the morning, when soberness returns, he is aghast to find himself in a mortuary of fire-worshipers, his couch a bier, and the form which he mistook for that of his bride the corpse of an old woman beginning to decay. On emerging from the mortuary with his garments all soiled, what is his shame to see his father, the king, approaching with a retinue of soldiers! Such is a feeble picture of the shame those will feel in the next world who in this have greedily abandoned themselves to what they thought were delights.

The third spiritual hell is that of disappointment and failure to reach the real object of existence. Man was intended to mirror forth the light of the knowledge of God, but if he arrives in the next world with his soul thickly coated with the rust of sensual indulgence he will entirely fail of the object for which he was made. His disappointment may be figured in the following way: Suppose a man is passing with some companions through a dark wood. Here and there, glimmering on the ground, lie variously colored stones. His companions collect and carry these and advise him to do the same. "For," say they, "we have heard that these stones will fetch a high price in the place whither we are going." He, on the other hand, laughs at them and calls them fools for leading themselves in the vain hope of gain while he walks free and unencumbered. Presently they emerge into the full daylight and find that these colored stones are rubies, emeralds, and other jewels of priceless value. The man's disappointment and chagrin at not having gathered some when so easily within his reach may be more easily imagined than described. Such will be the remorse of those hereafter, who, while passing through this world, have been at no pains to acquire the jewels of virtue and the treasures of religion.

This journey of man through the world may be divided into four stages—the sensuous, the experimental, the instinctive, the rational. In the first he is like a moth which, though it has sight, has no memory, and will singe itself again and again at the same candle. In the second stage he is like a dog which, having once been beaten, will run away at the sight of a stick. In the third he is like a horse or a sheep, both of which instinctively fly at the sight of a lion or wolf, their natural enemies, while they will not fly from a camel or a buffalo, though these last are much greater in size. In the fourth stage man altogether transcends the limits of the animals and becomes capable, to some extent, of foreseeing and providing for the future. His movements at first may be compared to ordinary walking on land, then to traversing the sea in a ship, then, on the fourth plane, where he is conversant with realities, to walking on the sea, while beyond this plane there is a fifth, known to the prophets and saints, whose progress may be compared to flying through the air.

Thus man is capable of existing on several different planes from the animal to the angelic, and precisely in this lies his danger, i. e., of falling to the very lowest. In the Koran it is written, "We proposed the burden (i.e., responsibility or free-will) to the heavens and the earth and the mountains, and they refused to undertake it. But man took it upon himself: Verily he is ignorant."[14] Neither animals nor angels can change their appointed rank and place. But man may sink to the animal or soar to the angel, and this is the meaning of his undertaking that "burden" of which the Koran speaks. The majority of men choose to remain in the two lower stages mentioned above, and the stationary are always hostile to the travellers or pilgrims, whom they far outnumber.

Many of the former class, having no fixed convictions about the future world, when mastered by their sensual appetites, deny it altogether. They say that hell is merely an invention of theologians to frighten people, and they regard theologians themselves with thinly veiled contempt. To argue with fools of this kind is of very little use. This much, however, may be said to such a man, with the possible result of making him pause and reflect: "Do you really think that the hundred and twenty-four thousand[15] prophets and saints who believed in the future life were all wrong and you are right in denying it?" If he replies, "Yes! I am as sure as I am that two are more than one, that there is no soul and no future life of joy and penalty," then the case of such a man is hopeless; all one can do is to leave

[14] Koran, 33:72. The term given here as "burden" is more often translated as "trust." It is also far from clear that what is meant by "burden" is free-will as the translator has interpolated; more conservative commentators often interpret it to mean the ritual obligations imposed on believers.

[15] See above, Introduction, n. 2.

him alone, remembering the words of the Koran, "Though thou call them to the right way, they will not be guided."[16]

But, should he say that a future life is possible but that the doctrine is so involved in doubt and mystery that it is impossible to decide whether it be true or not, then one may say to him: "Then you had better give it the benefit of the doubt! Suppose you are about to eat food and someone tells you a serpent has spat venom on it, you would probably refrain and rather endure the pangs of hunger than eat it, though your informant may be in jest or lying. Or suppose you are ill and a charm-writer says, "Give me a dirham[17] and I will write a charm which you can tie round your neck and which will cure you," you would probably give the dirham on the chance of deriving benefit from the charm. Or if an astrologer says, "When the moon has entered a certain constellation, drink such and such a medicine, and you will recover," though you may have very little faith in astrology, you very likely would try the experiment on the chance that he might be right. And do you not think that reliance is as well placed on the words of all the prophets, saints, and holy men, convinced as they were of a future life, as on the promise of a charm-writer or an astrologer? People take perilous voyages in ships for the sake of merely probable profit, and will you not suffer a little pain of abstinence now for the sake of eternal joy hereafter?

The Lord ᶜAlî[18] once, in arguing with an unbeliever, said, "If you are right, then neither of us will be any the worse in the future, but if we are right, then we shall escape, and you will

---

[16] Koran, 18:57. I have slightly altered Field's translation of this verse.

[17] Literally a "dram of silver" (*diram-i sîm*) or a drachma; Field translates it as "rupee."

[18] ᶜAlî b. Abî Tâlib was the Prophet Muḥammad's cousin and son-in-law and the fourth caliph (35-40/656-660). He is celebrated by both Sufis and Shiʿites for his valor and piety.

suffer."[19] This he said not because he himself was in any doubt, but merely to make an impression on the unbeliever. From all that we have said it follows that man's chief business in this world is to prepare for the next. Even if he is doubtful about a future existence, reason suggests that he should act as if there were one, considering the tremendous issues at stake. Peace be on those who follow the instruction!

[This concluded the introductory material of the Persian text. It was followed by the "first cornerstone" of the text, ten chapters dealing with the various aspects of "worship" (*ᶜibâdât*): faith, knowledge, purity, prayer, almsgiving, fasting, pilgrimage, Koran recitation, reciting the names of God, and a special type of private prayers (*awrâd*). In the next ten chapters, which made up the "second cornerstone" of the book, Ghazzâlî turned his attention to various practical matters (*muᶜâmilât*) in everyday life and how the pious Muslim should deal with them. Two of these chapters, dealing with marriage and the use of music, are translated here.]

---

[19] Many readers will recognize this as the "wager" proposed by the French philosopher Blaise Pascal. It has been shown that Pascal was familiar with the work of Ghazzâlî and probably derived his argument from this text: See M. Asín Palacios, *Los precedentes musulmanes del 'Pari' de Pascal* (Santander, 1920).

Chapter Five
Marriage as a Help or Hindrance to the Religious Life

[This was chapter VII in the original Field translation. It has been moved here and renumbered as chapter V so that the sequence of chapters will approximate the arrangement in the Persian text of the *Alchemy*. There, it constitutes the second chapter of the "third cornerstone."]

Marriage plays such a large part in human affairs that it must necessarily be taken into account in treating of the religious life and be regarded in both its aspects of advantage and disadvantage.

Seeing that God, as the Koran says, "only created men and genii for the purpose of worshiping,"[1] the first and obvious advantage of marriage is that the worshipers of God may increase in number. Theologians have therefore laid it down as a maxim that it is better to be engaged in matrimonial duties than in supererogatory devotions.

Another advantage of marriage is that, as the Prophet said, the prayers of children profit their parents when the latter are dead, and children who die before their parents intercede for them on the Day of Judgment. "When a child," said the Prophet, "is told to enter heaven, it weeps and says, 'I will not enter in without my father and mother.'" Again, one day the

---

[1] Koran, 51:56.

Prophet seized hold of a man's sleeves and drew him violently towards himself, saying, "Even thus shall children draw their parents into heaven." He added, "Children crowd together at the gate of heaven and cry out for their fathers and mothers, till those of the latter who are outside are told to enter in and join their children."

It is related of a certain celibate saint that he once dreamt that the Judgment Day had come. The sun had approached close to the earth and people were perishing of thirst: a crowd of boys were moving about giving them water out of gold and silver vessels. But when the saint asked for water he was repulsed, and one of the boys said to him, "Not one of us here is your son." As soon as the saint awoke he made preparations to marry.

Another advantage of marriage is that to sit with and be friendly to one's wife is a relaxation for the mind after being occupied in religious duties, and after such relaxation one may return to one's devotions with renewed zest. Thus the Prophet himself, when he found the weight of his revelations press too heavily upon him touched his wife ᶜÂ'isha[2] and said, "Speak to me, O ᶜÂ'isha, speak to me!" This he did that, from that familiar human touch, he might receive strength to support fresh revelations. For a similar reason he used to bid the

---

[2] ᶜÂ'isha, daughter of Abû Bakr (on whom see below, n. 3), was born in Mecca around 614; she was betrothed to Muḥammad at age six or seven, but the marriage was not consummated until she was nine. She came to be regarded as the prophet's favorite among the various women he married following the death of his first wife Khadîja. ᶜÂ'isha played a prominent role in many events after the prophet's death, including participation in a major revolt against the caliph ᶜAlî in 35/656. She died in 58/678. Many traditions of the prophet are related on the authority of ᶜÂ'isha and her memory is highly venerated among Sunnî Muslims, but Shi'ites disparage her because of her unrelenting enmity towards the house of ᶜAlî. An excellent modern biography of her is Nabia Abbott, *Aisha, the Beloved of Mohammed* (Chicago, 1942).

Muezzin Bilâl[3] give the call to prayer, and sometimes he used to smell sweet perfumes. It is a well-known saying of his, "I have loved three things in the world: perfumes, and women, and refreshment in prayer."[4] One one occasion ᶜUmar[5] asked the Prophet what were the things specially to be sought in the world. He answered, "A tongue occupied in the remembering of God, a grateful heart, and a believing wife."

A further advantage of marriage is that there should be someone to take care of the house, cook the food, wash the dishes, and sweep the floor, etc. If a man is busy in such work he cannot acquire learning, or carry on his business, or engage in his devotions properly. For this reason Abû Sulaymân[6] has said, "A good wife is not a blessing of this world merely, but of the next, because she provides a man leisure in which to think of the next world;" and one of the Caliph ᶜUmar's sayings is "After faith, no blessing is equal to a good wife."

Marriage has, moreover, this good in it, that to be patient with feminine peculiarities, to provide the necessaries which wives require, and to keep them in the path of the law, is a very important part of religion. The Prophet said, "To give one's

---

[3] Bilâl b. Rabâḥ (d. 20/641 or a little later) was an Ethiopian slave who was one of the earliest converts to Islam and who suffered much persecution for his faith. When the Prophet Muḥammad introduced the practice of the *adhân*, or summons to ritual prayer, he entrusted the responsibility of chanting it to Bilâl because of the strength and clarity of his voice. He was thus the first muezzin (*mu'adhdhin*) in Islam.

[4] This is a relatively famous *ḥadîth*. In some cases, the love of horses is added to (or substituted for) the love of prayer. See al-Nasâ'î, *Sunan* (Cairo, 1313/1895), 28/2, 36/1.

[5] ᶜUmar b. al-Khaṭṭâb was one of Muḥammad's closest associates and the second caliph, who ruled during the period of the most spectacular Arab conquests and who laid the foundations of the Islamic empire. He was assassinated in 23/644.

[6] Probably Abû Sulaymân al-Dârânî, a disciple of Ḥasan al-Baṣrî in Syria (d. 215/830); he is frequently cited by Ghazzâlî in the *Iḥyâ'*.

wife the money she requires is more important than to give alms." Once, when Ibn al-Mubârak[7] was engaged in a campaign against the infidels, one of his companions asked him, "Is any work more meritorious than religious war?" "Yes," he replied, "to feed and clothe one's wife and children properly." The celebrated saint Bishr Ḥâfî[8] said, "It is better that a man should work for wife and children than merely for himself."[9] In the Traditions it has been recorded that some sins can only be atoned for by enduring trouble for the sake of one's family.[10]

Concerning a certain saint it is related that his wife died and he would not marry again, though people urged him, saying it was easier to concentrate his thoughts in solitude. One night he saw in a dream the door of heaven opened and numbers of angels descending. They came near and looked upon him, and one said, "Is this that selfish wretch?" and his fellow answered, "Yes, this is he." The saint was too alarmed to ask whom they meant, but presently a boy passed and he asked him. "It is you they are speaking about," replied the boy; "only up to a week ago your good works were being recorded in heaven along with those of other saints, but now they have erased your name from the roll." Greatly disturbed in mind as

---

[7] The reference is probably to the Khurâsânî collector of *ḥadith*s and author of a book on asceticism, ᶜAbd Allah b. al-Mubârak (d. 181/797). See EI_2, 3:879. An English translation of a traditional biography of him (as found in ᶜAṭṭâr's *Tadhkirat al-Awliyâ'*) is given in A. J. Arberry, *Muslim Saints and Mystics* (London, 1966), pp. 124-28.

[8] Bishr b. al-Ḥârith (d. ca. 226/840), known as al-Ḥâfî ("the Barefoot") was a Sufi from Marw in eastern Iran who moved to Baghdad and taught the importance of *ikhlâṣ*, sincerity, in thought and deed. See EI_2, 1:1244-46; Arberry, *Saints and Mystics,* pp. 80-86.

[9] This is somewhat altered from the Persian text, where Bishr attributes this virtue to the traditionist and conservative legal scholar Aḥmad b. Ḥanbal.

[10] The responsibility of providing for the material needs of one's wife and children is known as *nafaqa*; under Islamic law, it is absolutely obligatory upon the husband.

soon as he awoke, he hastened to be married. From all the above considerations it will be seen that marriage is desirable.

We come now to treat of the drawbacks to marriage. One of these is that there is a danger, especially in the present time, that a man should gain a livelihood by unlawful means in order to support his family, and no amount of good works can compensate for this. The Prophet said that at the resurrection a certain man with a whole mountain-load of good works will be brought forward and stationed near the Balance.[11] He will then be asked, "By what means did you support your family?" He will not be able to give a satisfactory answer, and all his good works will be canceled, and proclamation will be made concerning him, "This is the man whose family have devoured all his good deeds!"

Another drawback to marriage is this, that to treat one's family kindly and patiently and to bring back their affairs to a satisfactory issue can only be done by those who have a good disposition. There is great danger lest a man should treat his family harshly, or neglect them, and so bring sin upon himself. The Prophet said, "He who deserts his wife and children is like a runaway slave; till he returns to them none of his fasts or prayers will be accepted by God." In brief, man has a lower nature, and, till he can control his own lower nature, he had better not assume the responsibility of controlling another's. Someone asked the saint Bishr Ḥâfî why he did not marry. "I am afraid," he replied, "of that verse in the Koran, 'The rights

[11] According to the Koran, 21:47, the *mîzân* or Balance (Persian text: *tirâz*) would be used on Judgment Day to weigh an individual's good and evil deeds. See Hughes, *Dictionary of Islam*, pp. 353-54 for further commentary on this verse.

of women over men are precisely the same as the rights of men over women.'"[12]

A third disadvantage of marriage is that the cares of a family often prevent a man from concentrating his thoughts on God and on a future life, and may, unless he is careful, lead to his destruction, for God has said, "Let not your riches and children turn you away from remembering God."[13] He who thinks he can concentrate himself better on his religious duties by not marrying had better remain single, and he who fears falling into sin if he does not marry, had better do so.

We now come to the qualities which should be sought in a wife.[14] The most important of all is chastity. If a wife is unchaste, and her husband keeps silent, he gets a bad name and is hindered in his religious life; if he speaks, his life becomes embittered; and if he divorces her, he may feel the pang of separation. A wife who is beautiful but of evil character is a great calamity; such a one had better be divorced. The Prophet said, "He who seeks a wife for the sake of her beauty or wealth will lose both."

The second desirable quality in a wife is a good disposition. An ill-tempered or ungrateful or loquacious or imperious wife makes existence unbearable, and is a great hindrance to leading a devout life.

The third quality to be sought is beauty, as this calls forth love and affection. Therefore one should see a woman before marrying her. The Prophet said, "The women of such a tribe have all a defect in their eyes; he who wishes to marry one

---

[12] The allusion is to the Koran, 2:228—"And women shall have rights similar to the rights against them" (i.e., that men have over them).

[13] Koran 63:9. Field mistakenly translates "riches and children" as "wives and children."

[14] In the Persian text, this is preceded by a discussion of the requirements for a legally valid marriage.

should see her first." The wise have said that he who marries a wife without seeing her is sure to repent it afterwards. It is true that one should not marry solely for the sake of beauty, but this does not mean that beauty should be reckoned of no account at all.

The fourth desirable point is that the sum paid by the husband as the wife's marriage-portion should be moderate. The Prophet said, "She is the best kind of wife whose marriage-portion is small, and whose beauty is great." He himself settled the marriage-portion of some women at ten dirhams,[15] and his own daughters' marriage-portions were not more than four hundred dirhams.

Fifthly, she should not be barren. "A piece of old matting lying in the corner of the house is better than a barren wife."[16]

Other qualities in a desirable wife are these: she should be of a good stock, not married previously, and not too nearly related to her husband.[17]

Regarding the Observances of Marriage[18]

Marriage is a religious institution, and should be treated in a religious way, otherwise the mating of men and women is not

[15] The *dirham* (Greek drachma) was a silver coin which usually weighed about 2.97 grams. See EI_2, 2:319-20.

[16] Another traditional saying attributed to Muḥammad.

[17] The Koran, 4:23, specified several degrees of blood kinship and foster relationships within which marriage was prohibited; apart from these limits, however, legally valid marriages could be, and often were, contracted between relatives as close as first cousins. Here Ghazzâlî is suggesting that marriage between people so closely related is to be discouraged, probably because of the inevitable family pressures that might distort the marital relationship. This paragraph is abridged from the Persian text, where each of these three qualities is treated separately and at greater length.

[18] The Persian text gives a list of twelve regulations for proper marriage etiquette; they are abridged and rearranged in Field's translation given here.

better than the mating of animals. The Law enjoins that there should be a feast on the occasion of every marriage.[19] When ᶜAbd al-Raḥman b. ᶜAwf[20] celebrated his marriage, the Prophet said to him, "Make a marriage-feast, even if you have only a goat to make it with." When the Prophet himself celebrated his marriage with Ṣafīya[21] he made a marriage-feast of dates and barley. It is also right that marriage should be accompanied with the beating of drums and of music, for man is the crown of creation.

Secondly, a man should remain on good terms with his wife. This does not mean that he should never cause her pains, but that he should bear any annoyance she causes him, whether by her unreasonableness or ingratitude, patiently. Woman is created weak, and requiring concealment; she should therefore be borne with patiently, and kept secluded. The Prophet said, "He who bears the ill-humor of his wife patiently will earn as much merit as Job did by the patient endurance of his trials." On his death-bed also he was heard to say, "Continue in prayer and treat your wives well, for they are your prisoners." He himself used to bear patiently the tempers of his wives. One

---

[19] Islamic marriage law required that at least one nuptial feast, the *walīma*, be provided, usually after the bride had gone to the groom's house and before the wedding night. People of all social standing should be invited, and an invitation to a wedding feast should always be accepted.

[20] ᶜAbd al-Raḥman b. ᶜAwf (d. 31/652) was an early convert to Islam and prominent political personality during the period of the first caliphs. He was one of ten people whom Muḥammad had promised would definitely be in Paradise.

[21] Ṣafīya, daughter of Ḥuyayy b. Akhṭab, was a Jewish woman of the tribe of Naḍīr captured after the fall of Khaybar in 7/628. The Prophet Muḥammad was so impressed by her beauty that he ransomed her, persuaded her to convert to Islam, and, after the execution of her husband, made her his eleventh wife. The hurriedness of the marriage arrangements, conducted on the way back to Medina after this battle, explains the simple nature of the bridal feast offered on this occasion.

day ᶜUmar's wife was angry and scolded him. He said to her, "Thou evil-tongued one, dost thou answer me back?" She replied, "Yes! the Lord of the prophets is better than thou, and his wives answer him back." He replied, "Alas for Ḥafṣa[22] if she does not humble herself;" and when he met her he said, "Take care not to answer the Prophet back." The Prophet also said, "The best of you is he who is best to his own family, as I am the best to mine."

Thirdly, a man should condescend to his wife's recreations and amusements, and not attempt to check them. The Prophet himself actually on one occasion ran races with his young wife ᶜÂ'isha. The first time he beat her, and the second time she beat him. Another time he held her up in his arms that she might look at some performing negroes. In fact, it would be difficult to find anyone who was so kind to his wives as the Prophet was to his. Wise men have said, "A man should come home smiling and eat what he finds and not ask for anything he does not find." However, he should not be over-indulgent, lest his wife lose her respect for him. If he sees anything plainly wrong on her part, he should not ignore but rebuke it, or he will become a laughing-stock. In the Koran it is written, "Men should have the upper hand over women,"[23] and the Prophet said, "Woe to the man who is the servant of his wife" for she should be his servant. Wise men have said, "Consult women, and act the contrary to what they advise."[24] In truth there is something perverse in women, and if they are allowed even a

---

[22] ᶜUmar's daughter and one of Muḥammad's wives. See EI_2, 3:63-65.

[23] Koran, 4:34. The phrase given here as "upper hand" (in Arabic *qawwâmûn*) is often translated in different ways such as the "superiors," "protectors," or "managers of the affairs" of women.

[24] This famous maxim is cited, for example, by Niẓâm al-Mulk, *The Book of Government or Rules for Kings* (translated by Hubert Darke; New Haven, 1960), pp. 188-189.

little license, they get out of control altogether, and it is difficult to reduce them to order again. In dealing with them one should endeavor to use a mixture of severity and tenderness, with a greater proportion of the latter. The Prophet said, "Woman was formed of a crooked rib; if you try to bend her, you will break her; if you leave her alone, she will grow more and more crooked; therefore treat her tenderly."[25]

As regards propriety, one cannot be too careful not to let one's wife look at or be looked at by a stranger, for the beginning of all mischief is in the eye. As far as possible, she should not be allowed out of the house, nor to go on the roof, nor to stand at the door. Care should be taken, however, not to be unreasonably jealous and strict. The Prophet one day asked his daughter Fâṭima, "What is the best thing for women?" She answered, "They should not look on strangers, nor strangers on them." The Prophet was pleased at this remark, and embraced her, saying, "Verily, thou art a piece of my liver!"[26] The Commander of the Faithful, ᶜUmar, said, "Don't give women fine clothes, for as soon as they have them they will want to go out of the house." In the time of the Prophet women had permission to go to the mosques and stand in the last row of the worshipers; but this was subsequently forbidden.

A man should keep his wife properly supplied with money, and not stint her. To give a wife her proper maintenance is more meritorious than to give alms. The Prophet said,

---

[25] This tradition is cited by Bukhârî, *Ṣaḥîḥ*, 67/80.

[26] In most Middle Eastern cultures, the liver is regarded much the way the heart is regarded in the West: It is a central and vital organ, and it is associated with feelings of joy, love, anger, and sorrow. To say "You are a part of my liver" is a common metaphor to mean that the person addressed is very dear. See the article "Kabid" in EI_2, 4:327-33. The Persian text, however, does not use this metaphor; it has the Prophet draw his daughter aside and quote a phrase from Koran 3:34, [we are] "offspring one of the other."

"Suppose a man spends one dînâr[27] in religious war, another in ransoming a slave, a third in charity, and gives the fourth to his wife, the giving of this last surpasses in merit all the others put together."

A man should not eat anything especially good by himself, or, if he has eaten it, he should keep silent about it and not praise it before his wife. It is better for husband and wife to eat together, if a guest be not present, for the Prophet said, "When they do so, God sends His blessing upon them, and the angels pray for them." The most important point to see is that the supplies given to one's wife are acquired by lawful means.

If a man's wife be rebellious and disobedient, he should at first admonish her gently; if this is not sufficient he should sleep in a separate chamber for three nights. Should this also fail he may strike her, but not on the mouth, nor with such force as to wound her.[28] Should she be remiss in her religious duties, he should manifest his displeasure to her for an entire month, as the Prophet did on one occasion to all his wives.

The greatest care should be taken to avoid divorce, for, though divorce is permitted, yet God disapproves of it, because the very utterance of the word "divorce" causes a woman pain, and how can it be right to pain anyone? When divorce is absolutely necessary, the formula for it should not be repeated thrice all at once but on three different occasions.[29] A woman

---

[27] The *dînâr* (Greek denarius) was a gold coin 4.25 to 4.55 grams in weight. See EI_2, 2:297-98.

[28] The Koranic advice (4:34) on disciplining wives is "admonish them (first); (next) refuse to share their beds, (And last) beat them (lightly)."

[29] In Islamic law, the most common form of divorce is known as *ṭalâq*, whereby the husband simply repeats three times the oath "You are divorced!" While it would be legal to repeat the phrase three times in succession, this is typically discouraged. Repeating the formula of divorce on three separate occasions would tend to prevent the husband from hastily divorcing his wife out

should be divorced kindly, not through anger and contempt, and not without reason. After divorce a man should give his former wife a present, and not tell others that she has been divorced for such and such a fault. Of a certain man who was instituting divorce-proceedings against his wife it is related that people asked him, "Why are you divorcing her?" He answered, "I do not reveal my wife's secrets." When he had actually divorced her, he was asked again, and said, "She is a stranger to me now; I have nothing to do with her private affairs."

Hitherto we have treated of the rights of the wife over her husband, but the rights of the husband over the wife are even more binding. The Prophet said, "If it were right to worship anyone except God, it would be right for wives to worship their husbands." A wife should not boast of her beauty before her husband, she should not requite his kindness with ingratitude, she should not say to him, "Why have you treated me thus and thus?" The Prophet said, "I looked into hell and saw many women there. I asked the reason, and received this reply, 'Because they abused their husbands and were ungrateful to them.'"

---

of anger and regretting it later. On ṭalâq, see the *Encyclopaedia of Islam* (first edition; Leiden, 1913-36), 4:636-40 (hereafter cited as EI_1).

Chapter Six
On Music and Dancing

[This was Chapter V in the Field translation; it is rearranged here to follow the chapter on marriage; in the Persian text of the *Alchemy*, it was the eighth chapter of the "second cornerstone," dealing with auditory and ecstatic mystical experience, *samâ*ᶜ and *wajd*.]

The heart of man has been so constituted by the Almighty that, like a flint, it contains a hidden fire which is evoked by music and harmony, and renders man beside himself with ecstasy. These harmonies are echoes of that higher world of beauty which we call the world of spirits, they remind man of his relationship to that world, and produce in him an emotion so deep and strange that he himself is powerless to explain it. The effect of music and dancing is deeper in proportion as the natures on which they act are simple and prone to emotion; they fan into a flame whatever love is already dormant in the heart, whether it be earthly and sensual, or divine and spiritual.

Accordingly there has been much dispute among theologians as to the lawfulness of music and dancing regarded as religious exercises. One sect, the Ẓâhirites,[1] holding that

---

[1] The Ẓâhirites represented a school of Muslim law founded by Da'ûd b. ᶜAlî b. Khalaf (d. 270/884). Most of its followers were in eastern Iran and Spain (notably Ibn Ḥazm). It was virtually extinct by the sixteenth century. A better translation for the name of this school of law would be "literalists" since they argued that religious law could be based only on literal readings of the texts of the Koran and the traditions of the Prophet Muḥammad. See I. Goldziher, *Die Ẓâhiriten. Ihr Lehrsystem und ihre Geschichte* (Leipzig, 1884).

God is altogether incommensurable with man, deny the possibility of man's really feeling love to God, and say that he can only love those of his own species. If he does feel what he thinks is love to his Creator they say it is a mere projection, or shadow cast by his own fantasy, or a reflection of love to the Creature; music and dancing, according to them, have only to do with creature love, and are therefore unlawful as religious exercises. If we ask them what is the meaning of that "love to God" which is enjoined by the religious law, they reply that it means obedience and worship. This is an error which we hope to confute in a later chapter dealing with the love of God. At present we content ourselves with saying that music and dancing do not put into the heart what is not there already, but only fan into a flame dormant emotions. Therefore if a man has in his heart that love to God which the law enjoins, it is perfectly lawful, nay, laudable in him to take part in exercises which promote it. On the other hand, if his heart is full of sensual desires, music and dancing will only increase them and are therefore unlawful for him. While, if he listens to them merely as a matter of amusement, they are neither lawful nor unlawful, but indifferent. For the mere fact that they are pleasant does not make them unlawful anymore than the pleasure of listening to the singing of birds or looking at green grass and running water is unlawful. The innocent character of music and dancing, regarded merely as a pastime, is also corroborated by an authentic tradition which we have from the Lady ᶜÂ'isha,[2] who narrates: "One festival-day some negroes were performing in a mosque. The Prophet said to me, 'Do you wish to see them?' I replied, 'Yes.' Accordingly he lifted me up with his own blessed hand, and I looked on so long that he said more than once, 'Haven't you had enough?'" Another tradition

---

[2] See above, Chapter Five, n. 2.

from the Lady ᶜÂ'isha is as follows: "One festival day two girls came to my house and began to play and sing. The Prophet came in and lay down on the couch, turning his face away. Presently Abû Bakr[3] entered, and seeing the girls playing, exclaimed, 'What! the pipe of Satan in the Prophet's house!' Whereupon the Prophet turned and said, 'Let them alone, Abû Bakr, for this is a festival-day.'"

Passing over the cases where music and dancing rouse into a flame evil desires already dormant in the heart, we come to those cases where they are quite lawful. Such are those of the pilgrims who celebrate the glories of the House of God at Mecca in song, and thus incite others to go on pilgrimage, and of minstrels whose music and songs stir up martial ardor in the breasts of their auditors and incite them to fight against infidels. Similarly, mournful music which excites sorrow for sin and failure in religious life is lawful; of this nature was the music of David. But dirges which increase sorrow for the dead are not lawful, for it is written in the Koran, "Despair not over what you have lost."[4] On the other hand, joyful music at weddings and feasts and on such occasions as a circumcision or the return from a journey is lawful.

We come now to the purely religious use of music and dancing: such is that of the Sufis who by this means stir up in themselves greater love towards God and, by means of music, often obtain spiritual visions and ecstasies, their heart becoming in this condition as clean as silver in the flame of a furnace, and attaining a degree of purity which could never be

---

[3] One of the very first converts to Islam and a close personal friend of Muḥammad, Abû Bakr was elected caliph immediately after Muḥammad's death in 11/632; he himself died in 13/634 after having successfully put down the revolts of the apostate Arab tribes and initiated the wars against the Byzantines and Sassanids in Syria and Iraq respectively.

[4] Koran, 57:23.

attained by any amount of mere outward austerities. The Sufi then becomes so keenly aware of his relationship to the spiritual world that he loses all consciousness of this world, and often falls down senseless.

It is not, however, lawful for the aspirant to Sufism to take part in this mystical dancing without the permission of his "Pîr," or spiritual director. It is related of the Shaykh Abu'l-Qâsim Gurgânî[5] that, when one of his disciples[6] requested leave to take part in such a dance, he said, "Keep a strict fast for three days; then let them cook for you tempting dishes; if then, you still prefer the dance, you may take part in it." The disciple, however, whose heart is not thoroughly purged from earthly desires, though he may have obtained some glimpse of the mystics' path, should be forbidden by his director to take part in such dances, as they will do him more harm than good.

Those who deny the reality of the ecstasies and other spiritual experiences of the Sufis merely betray their own narrow-mindedness and shallow insight. Some allowance, however, must be made for them, for it is as difficult to believe in the reality of states of which one has no personal experience as it is for a blind man to understand the pleasure of looking at green grass and running water, or for a child to comprehend the pleasure of exercising sovereignty. A wise man, though he himself may have no experience of those states, will not therefore deny their reality, for what folly can be greater than his who denies the reality of a thing merely because he himself has not experienced it! Of such people it is written in the

---

[5] Abu'l-Qâsim ʿAlî b. ʿAbd Allah al-Gurgânî, a well-known early Muslim mystic; see Abu'l-Ḥasan Hujwîrî, *Kashf al-maḥjûb*, translated by R. Nicholson *The Kashf al-maḥjûb, the Oldest Persian Treatise on Sufiism* (London, 1936), pp. 169-70 for a biographical notice.

[6] The Persian text gives the name of the disciple as Khᵛâjah ʿAlî Ḥallâj.

Koran, "Those who have not the guidance will say, 'This is a manifest imposture.'"[7]

As regards the erotic poetry which is recited in Sufi gatherings, and to which people sometimes make objection,[8] we must remember that, when in such poetry mention is made of separation from or union with the beloved, the Sufi, who is an adept in the love of God applies such expressions to separation from or union with Him. Similarly, "dark locks" are taken to signify the darkness of unbelief; "the brightness of the face," the light of faith; and "drunkenness" the Sufi's ecstasy. Take, for instance, the verse:

> Thou may'st measure out thousands of measures of wine,
> But, till thou drink it, no joy is thine.[9]

By this the writer means that the true delights of religion cannot be reached by way of formal instruction,[10] but by felt attraction and desire. A man may converse much and write volumes concerning love, faith, piety, and so forth, and blacken paper to any extent, but till he himself possesses these attributes all this will do him no good. Thus, those who find fault with the Sufis for being powerfully affected, even to ecstasy, by these and similar verses, are merely shallow and uncharitable. Even camels are sometimes so powerfully affected by the Arabic songs of their drivers that they will run

---

[7] Koran, 46:11.

[8] This section is much abridged; it deals with many of the objections of traditional religious scholars to ecstatic mystical experience.

[9] This verse also appears in Ghazzâlî's *Ayyuhâ al-walad*; see George Scherer, *O Youth!* (Beirut, 1933), p. 55. Interestingly, in that Arabic text the verse is also quoted in Persian.

[10] A more literal translation of this passage would be that religious understanding cannot be based only on *ḥadîth* and *ᶜilm*.

rapidly, bearing heavy burdens, till they fall down in a state of exhaustion.

The Sufi hearer, however, is in danger of blasphemy if he applies some of the verses which he hears to God. For instance, if he hears such a verse as "Thou art changed from thy former inclination," he must not apply it to God, who cannot change, but to himself and his own variations of mood. God is like the sun, which is always shining, but sometimes for us His light is eclipsed by some object which intervenes between us and Him.

Regarding some adepts it is related that they attain to such a degree of ecstasy that they lose themselves in God. Such was the case with Shaykh Abu'l-Ḥusayn Nûrî,[11] who, on hearing a certain verse, fell into an ecstatic condition, and, coming into a field full of stalks of newly cut sugar-canes, ran about till his feet were wounded and bleeding, and, not long afterwards, expired. In such cases some have supposed that there occurs an actual descent of Deity into humanity, but this would be as great a mistake as that of one who, having for the first time seen his reflection in a mirror, should suppose that, somehow or other, he had become incorporated with the mirror, or that the red-and-white hues which the mirror reflects were qualities inherent in it.

The states of ecstasy into which the Sufis fall vary according to the emotions which pre-dominate in them—love, fear, desire, repentance, etc. These states, as we have mentioned above, are often the result not only of hearing verses of the

---

[11] Field has Abu'l-Hassan Nuri. Shaykh Abu'l-Ḥusayn (or Abu'l-Ḥasan) Nûrî was a famous mystic of Baghdad (d. 295/907-8), noted for his claim to be "a lover of God," who inspired his own order of Sufism; see Hujwîrî/Nicholson, *Kashf al-maḥjûb*, pp. 130-32, 189-95; Arberry, *Saints and Mystics*, pp. 221-30 (which gives this same anecdote); Smith, *Early Mystic*, p. 31; Schimmel, *Mystical Dimensions*, pp. 60-61.

Koran, but erotic poetry. Some have objected to the reciting of poetry, as well as of the Koran, on these occasions; but it should be remembered that all the verses of the Koran are not adapted to stir the emotions—such, for instance, as that which commands that a man should leave his mother the sixth part of his property and his sister the half, or that which orders that a widow must wait four months after the death of her husband before becoming espoused to another man. The natures which can be thrown into religious ecstasy by the recital of such verses are peculiarly sensitive and very rare.

Another reason for the use of poetry as well as of the Koran on these occasions is that people are so familiar with the Koran, many even knowing it by heart, that the effect of it has been dulled by constant repetition. One cannot be always quoting new verses of the Koran as one can of poetry. Once, when some wild Arabs were hearing the Koran for the first time and were strongly moved by it, Abû Bakr said to them, "We were once like you, but our hearts have grown hard," meaning that the Koran loses some of its effect on those familiar with it. For the same reason the Caliph ᶜUmar used to command the pilgrims to Mecca to leave it quickly. "For," he said, "I fear if you grow too familiar with the Holy City the awe of it will depart from your hearts."[12]

There is, moreover, something pertaining to the light and frivolous, at least in the eyes of any common people, in the use of singing and musical instruments, such as the pipe and drum, and it is not befitting that the majesty of the Koran should be, even temporarily, associated with these things. It is related of the Prophet that once, when he entered the house of Rabiᶜa,

[12] This tradition is reported by Bukhârî, *Ṣaḥîḥ*, 63/47; Muslim, *Ṣaḥîḥ* 15/441-44; and other authorities.

the daughter of Muᶜâdh,[13] some singing-girls who were there began extemporizing in his honor. He abruptly bade them cease, as the praise of the Prophet was too sacred a theme to be treated in that way. There is also some danger, if verses of the Koran are exclusively used, that the hearers should attach to them some private interpretations of their own, and this is unlawful. On the other hand, no harm attaches to interpreting lines of poetry in various ways, as it is not necessary to apply to a poem the same meaning which the author had.

Other features of these mystic dances are the bodily contortions and tearing of clothes with which they are sometimes accompanied. If these are the result of genuine ecstatic conditions there is nothing to be said against them, but if they are self-conscious and deliberate on the part of those who wish to appear "adepts," then they are merely acts of hypocrisy. In any case the more perfect adept is he who controls himself till he is absolutely obliged to give vent to his feelings. It is related of a certain youth who was a disciple of Shaykh Junayd[14] that, on hearing singing commence in an assembly of the Sufis, he could not restrain himself, but began to shriek in ecstasy. Junayd said to him, "If you do that again, don't remain in my company." After this the youth used to restrain himself on such occasions, but at last one day his emotions were so powerfully stirred that, after long and forcible repression of them, he uttered a shriek and died.

---

[13] The daughter of one of the companions of the Prophet Muḥammad; her biography is in Ibn Saᶜd, *al-Ṭabaqât al-kabîr* (Beirut, 1957-68), 8:447-48.

[14] Abu'l-Qâsim al-Junayd (d. 298/910) was one of the most famous of all Sufi teachers; see Arberry, *Saints and Mystics*, pp. 192-213; A. H. Abdel-Kader, *The Life, Personality and Writings of al-Junayd* (London, 1962). Like Ghazzâlî, he encouraged the practice of the mysticism of "sobriety," a non-pantheistic and non-antinomian form of Sufism; this attitude is clearly reflected in the anecdote related here.

To conclude: In holding these assemblies, regard must be had to time and place, and that no spectators come from unworthy motives. Those who participate in them should sit in silence, not looking at one another, but keeping their heads bent, as at prayer, and concentrating their minds on God. Each should watch for whatever may be revealed to his own heart, and not make any movements from mere self-conscious impulse. But if anyone of them stands up in a state of genuine ecstasy all the rest should stand up with him, and if any one's turban falls off the others should also lay their turbans down.

Although these matters are comparative novelties in Islam and have not been received from the first followers of the Prophet, we must remember that all novelties are not forbidden, but only those which directly contravene the Law. For instance, the *tarâwiḥ* or night-prayer was first instituted by the Caliph ᶜUmar.[15] The Prophet said, "Live with each man according to his habits and disposition," therefore it is right to fall in with usages that please people, when non-conformity would vex them. It is true that the Companions were not in the habit of rising on the entrance of the Prophet, as they disliked this practice; but where it has become established, and abstaining from it would cause annoyance, it is better to conform to it. The Arabs have their own customs, and the Persians have theirs, and God knoweth which is best.[16]

---

[15] The *tarâwîḥ* are special prayer sections recited each night during the month of Ramadan at the end of the regular night ritual prayers. Although practiced during the lifetime of the Prophet Muḥammad, it was ᶜUmar who first organized them on a regular basis. They are described in detail by Bukhârî; see also EI_1, 4:665.

[16] This is an interesting example of Ghazzâlî's tolerance, which should be understood against the background of both the ethnic controversy between the Arabs and Persians in early Islam (known as the *shuᶜûbiyya*) and the debate over the validity of customary law or practice (*ᶜadât*) when it conflicts with traditional religious law.

[The "third cornerstone" of Ghazzâlî's book dealt with various attitudes and activities which inhibit spiritual progress and ultimately lead to damnation. These include such things as concupiscence, worldliness, avarice, and pride. Then, in the fourth and final "cornerstone" Ghazzâlî explains the "remedies" or spiritual practices which can lead to salvation. Two of these chapters form the conclusion of this translation.]

Chapter Seven
The Recollection of God

[This was Chapter VI in the Field translation; it is moved here to conform to the sequence of the Persian text, where it is the sixth chapter of the "fourth cornerstone." In Ghazzâlî's terminology the qualities mentioned in the title are known as *muhâsiba* and *murâqiba*. They are inspired by some of the "beautiful names" or attributes of God: *al-Ḥasîb* or *al-Muḥtasib* ("The One Who Demands an Account") and *al-Raqîb* ("The One Who Watches"). The idea which Ghazzâlî develops is that one should evaluate one's actions with a view to accounting for them to God and always remembering that God is watching whatever one does.]

Know, O brother, that in the Koran God hath said, "We will set up a just balance on the Day of Resurrection, and no soul shall be wronged in anything. Whosoever has wrought a grain of good or ill shall then behold it."[1] In the Koran it is also written, "Let every soul see what it sends on before it for the Day of Account."[2] It was a saying of the Caliph ʿUmar, "Call yourselves to account before ye be called to account;" and God says, "O ye believers, be patient and strive [against your natural desires], and maintain the strife

[1] Koran, 21:47. Field's translation of the verse is kept here; ʿAlî translates it, "We shall set up scales of justice for the day of Judgment, so that not a soul will be dealt with unjustly in the least. And if there be (no more than) the weight of a mustard seed, We will bring it (to account): And enough are We to take account."

[2] A rather free translation of Koran, 59:18: "...let every soul look to what it has sent forth for the morrow."

manfully."[3] The saints have always understood that they have come into this world to carry on a spiritual traffic, the resulting gain or loss of which is heaven or hell. They have, therefore, always kept a jealous eye upon the flesh, which, like a treacherous partner in business, may cause them great loss. He, therefore, is a wise man who, after his morning prayer, spends a whole hour in making a spiritual reckoning, and says to his soul, "Oh my soul, thou hast only one life; no single moment that has passed can be recovered for in the counsel of God the number of breaths allotted thee is fixed, and cannot be increased. When life is over no further spiritual traffic is possible for thee; therefore what thou dost, do now; treat this day as if thy life had been already spent, and this were an extra day granted thee by the special favor of the Almighty. What can be greater folly than to lose it?"

At the resurrection a man will find all the hours of his life arranged like a long series of treasure-chests. The door of one will be opened, and it will be seen to be full of light; it represents an hour which he spent in doing good. His heart will be filled with such joy that even a fraction of it would make the inhabitants of hell forget the fire. The door of a second will be opened; it is pitch-dark within, and from it issues such an evil odor as will cause every one to hold his nose; it represents an hour which he spent in ill-doing, and he will suffer such terror that a fraction of it would embitter Paradise for the blessed. The door of a third treasure-chest will be opened; it will be seen to be empty and neither light or dark within: this represents the hour in which he did neither good nor evil. Then he will feel remorse and confusion like that of a man who has been the possessor of a great treasure and wasted it or let it slip from his grasp. Thus the whole series of the hours of his

[3] Koran, 3:200. The phrase in brackets was interpolated by the translator.

life will be displayed, one by one, to his gaze. Therefore a man should say to his soul every morning, "God has given thee twenty-four treasures; take heed lest thou lose anyone of them, for thou wilt not be able to endure the regret that will follow such loss."

The saints have said, "Even suppose God should forgive thee, after a wasted life, thou wilt not attain to the ranks of the righteous and must deplore thy loss; therefore keep a strict watch over thy tongue, thine eye, and each of thy seven members, for each of these is, as it were, a possible gate to hell. Say to thy flesh, 'If thou art rebellious, verily I will punish thee;' for, though the flesh is headstrong, it is capable of receiving instruction, and can be tamed by austerity." Such, then, is the aim of self-examination, and the Prophet had said, "Happy is he who does now that which will benefit him after death."

We come now to the recollection of God. This consists in a man's remembering that God observes all his acts and thoughts. People only see the outward, while God sees both the outer and the inner man. He who really believes this will have both his outer and inner being well disciplined. If he disbelieves it, he is an infidel, and if, while believing it, he acts contrary to the belief, he is guilty of the grossest presumption. One day a negro came to the Prophet and said, "O Prophet of God! I have committed much sin. Will my repentance be accepted, or not?" The Prophet said, "Yes." Then the negro said, "O Prophet of God, all the time I was committing sin, did God really behold it?" "Yes," was the answer. The negro uttered a cry and fell lifeless. Till a man is thoroughly convinced of the fact that he is always under God's observation it is impossible for him to act rightly.

A certain shaykh once had a disciple whom he favored above his other disciples, thus exciting their envy. One day the shaykh gave each of them a fowl and told each to go and kill it in a place where no one could see him. Accordingly each killed his fowl in some retired spot and brought it back, with the exception of the shaykh's favorite disciple, who brought his back alive, saying, "I have found no such place, for God sees everywhere." The shaykh said to the others, "You see now this youth's real rank; he has attained to the constant remembrance of God."

When Zulaykhâ tempted Joseph[4] she cast a cloth over the face of the idol she used to worship. Joseph said to her, "O Zulaykhâ, thou art ashamed before a block of stone, and should I not be ashamed before Him Who created the seven heavens and the earth?"

A man once came to the saint Junayd[5] and said, "I cannot keep my eyes from casting lascivious looks. How shall I do so?" "By remembering," Junayd answered, "that God sees you much more clearly than you see anyone else." In the traditions it is written that God has said, "Paradise is for those who intend to commit some sin and then remember that My eye is upon them and forbear."

ᶜAbdallah b. Dînâr[6] relates, "Once I was walking with the Caliph ᶜUmar near Mecca when we met a shepherd's slave-boy driving his flock. ᶜUmar said to him, 'Sell me a sheep.' The boy answered, 'They are not mine, but my master's.' Then, to try him, ᶜUmar said, 'Well, you can tell him that a wolf carried one

[4] An account of Joseph, who was renowned for his physical beauty, constitutes Chapter XII of the Koran and is regarded by many Muslims as the finest of the stories about the prophets. The story of his attempted seduction by his master's wife is found in the Koran, 12:23-29. In later tradition, the woman was given the name Zulaykhâ. The legend of her infatuation with Joseph became an especially popular subject for treatment by various Muslim poets.

[5] See above, Chapter Six, n. 14.

[6] Apparently the early, but rather obscure, traditionist ᶜAbdallah b. Dînâr al-Bahrânî; see Ibn Ḥajr, *Tahdhîb al-tahdhîb* (Haydarabad, 1325-27/1907-9), 5:203.

off, and he will know nothing about it.' 'No, he won't,' said the boy, 'but God will.' ᶜUmar then wept, and sending for the boy's master, purchased him and set him free, exclaiming, 'For this saying thou art free in this world and shalt be free in the next.'"

There are two degrees of this recollection of God. The first degree is that of those saints whose thoughts are altogether absorbed in the contemplation of the majesty of God, and have no room in their hearts for anything else at all. This is the lower degree of recollection for when a man's heart is fixed and his limbs are so controlled by his heart that they abstain from even lawful actions, he has no need of any device or safeguard against sins. It was to this kind of recollection that the Prophet referred when he said, "He who rises in the morning with only God in his mind, God shall look after him, both in this world and the next."

Some of these recollectors of God are so absorbed in the thought of Him that, if people speak to them, they do not hear, or walk in front of them they do not see, but stumble as if they collided with a wall. A certain saint relates as follows: "One day I passed by a place where archers were having a shooting-match. Some way off a man was sitting alone. I approached him and attempted to engage him in talk, but he replied, 'The remembrance of God is better than talk.' I said, 'Are you not lonely?' 'No,' he answered, 'God and two angels are with me.' Pointing to the archers, I asked, 'Which of these has carried off the prize?' 'That one,' was his reply, 'to whom God has allotted it.' Then I inquired, 'Where does this road come from?' Upon which, lifting up his eyes to heaven, he rose and departed, saying, 'O Lord! many of Thy creatures hold one back from the remembrance of Thee!'"

The saint Shiblî[7] one day went to see Abu'l-Ḥusayn Nûrî;[8] he found him sitting so still in contemplation that not a hair of his body moved. He asked him, "From whom didst thou learn to practice such fixity of contemplation?" Nûrî answered, "From a cat which I saw waiting at a mouse-hole in an attitude of even greater fixity than this." [A]bû ᶜAbd Allah [Ibn] Khafîf[9] relates, "I was informed that in the city of Ṣûr[10] a shaykh and his disciple were always sitting lost in the recollection of God. I went there and found them both sitting with their faces turned in the direction of Mecca. I saluted them thrice, but they gave no answer. I said, 'I adjure you by God to return my salutation.'[11] The youth raised his head and replied, 'O Ibn Khafîf! The world lasts but for a little time, and of this little time only a little is remaining. Thou art hindering us by

---

[7] Abû Bakr Dulaf b. Jaḥdar al-Shiblî (247/861-334/945) was a famous mystic from Baghdad, where his tomb is still venerated. He was a friend of the great Sufi martyr al-Ḥallâj; see Massignon/Mason, *The Passion of al-Ḥallâj*, 1:82-88; Schimmel, *Mystical Dimensions*, pp. 77-80; Arberry, *Saints and Mystics*, pp. 277-86 (the anecdote about Nûrî may also be found there, p. 228).

[8] The Field translation has "the Sufi Thawri," an apparent mistake for Sufyân al-Thawrî, a famous traditionist and ascetic. However, the Persian text, as well as the Arabic text found in the *Iḥyâ'*, 4:340, give the name as Abu'l-Ḥusayn Nûrî (see above, Chapter Six, n. 11). Owing the similarity of Nûrî and Thawrî in the Arabic script, the names are easily confused. The reading here is thus corrected to conform to the Persian text.

[9] Field has Ibn Ḥanif; this is corrected throughout this paragraph to conform to the correct name, Abû ᶜAbd Allah Muḥammad b. Khafîf as found in the Persian text. Ibn Khafîf (d. 371/982) was a famous Sufi from Shiraz, supposedly descended from an Iranian royal family. See Arberry, *Saints and Mystics*, pp. 257-63; Annemarie Schimmel, "Ibn Khafîf, an Early Representative of Sufism," *Journal of the Pakistan Historical Society* (1959); EI_2, 3:823-24.

[10] The city of Tyre in Lebanon; in Arberry, *Saints and Mystics*, p. 259 this anecdote is set in Egypt, not Tyre.

[11] The Koran, 4:86 admonishes believers, "When ye are saluted with a salutation, salute the person with a better than his or at least return it." It is thus regarded as extremely rude not to respond to such a greeting.

requiring us to return thy salutation.' He then bent his head again and was silent. I was angry and thirsty at the time, but the sight of those two quite carried me out of myself. I remained standing and prayed with them the afternoon and evening prayer. I then asked them for some spiritual advice. The younger replied, 'O Ibn Khafîf, we are afflicted; we do not possess that tongue which gives advice.' I remained standing there three days and nights; no word passed between us and none of us slept. Then I said within myself, 'I will adjure them by God to give me some counsel.' The younger, divining my thoughts, again raised his head: 'Go and seek such a man, the visitation of whom will bring God to thy remembrance and infix His fear in thy heart, and he will give thee that counsel which is conveyed by silence and not by speech.'" Such is the "recollection" of the saints which consists in being entirely absorbed in the contemplation of God.

The second degree of the recollection of God is that of "the companions of the right hand."[12] These are aware that God knows all about them, and feel abashed in His presence, yet they are not carried out of themselves by the thought of His majesty, but remain clearly conscious of themselves and of the world. Their condition is like that of a man who should be suddenly surprised in a state of nakedness and should hastily cover himself, while the other class resemble one who suddenly finds himself in the presence of the King and is confused and awe struck. The former subject every project which enters their minds to a thorough scrutiny, for at the Last Day three

---

[12] This metaphor for the righteous is derived from a somewhat cryptic passage in the Koran, 56:7-10 describing the Day of Judgment: "...Ye shall be sorted out into three classes. Then (there will be) the Companions of the Right Hand;—What will be the Companions of the Right Hand? And the Companions of the Left Hand,—What will be the Companions of the Left Hand? And those Foremost (in Faith) will be Foremost (in the Hereafter)."

questions will be asked respecting every action: the first, "Why did you do this?" the second, "In what way did you do this?" the third, "For what purpose did you do this?" The first will be asked because a man should act from divine and not merely Satanic or fleshly impulse. If this question is satisfactorily answered, the second will test in what way the action was done, wisely or carelessly and negligently, and the third, whether it was done simply to please God, or to gain the approval of men. If a man understands the meaning of these questions he will be very watchful over the state of his heart, and how he entertains thoughts which are likely to end in action. Rightly to discriminate among such thoughts is a very difficult and delicate matter and he who is not capable of it should attach himself to some spiritual director, intercourse with whom may illuminate his heart. He should avoid with the utmost care the merely worldly learned man who is an agent of Satan. God said to David,[13] "O David! ask no questions of the learned man who is intoxicated with love of the world, for he will rob thee of My love," and the Prophet said: "God loves that man who is keen to discern in doubtful things, and who suffers not his reason to be swayed by the assaults of passion." Reason and discrimination are closely connected, and he in whom reason does not rule passion will not be keen to discriminate.

Besides such cautious discrimination before acting a man should call himself strictly to account for his past actions. Every evening he should examine his heart as to what he has done to see whether he has gained or lost in his spiritual capital. This is the more necessary as the heart is like a treacherous business partner, always ready to cajole and deceive; sometimes it

---

[13] These revelations or inspirations (*waḥy*) sent to David are probably taken from a Muslim version of the Psalms known as the *Zabûr*, one of the various *Anecdotes of the Prophets* (*Qiṣaṣ al-anbiyâ'*) or perhaps from a now lost *Accounts of David* (*Akhbâr Dâ'ûd*) known to Ghazzâlî.

presents its own selfishness under the guise of obedience to God, so that a man supposes he has gained, whereas he has really lost.

A certain saint named Ibn al-Ṣimma,[14] sixty years of age, counted up the days of his life. He found they amounted to twenty-one thousand six hundred days. He said to himself, "Alas! if I have committed one sin every day, how can I escape from the load of twenty-one thousand six hundred sins?" He uttered a cry and fell to the ground; when they came to raise him they found him dead. But most people are heedless, and never think of calling themselves to account. If for every sin a man committed he placed a stone in an empty house, he would soon find that house full of stones; if his recording angels[15] demanded wages of him for writing down his sins, all his money would soon be gone. People count on their rosaries[16] with self-satisfaction the numbers of times they have recited the name of God, but they keep no rosary for reckoning the numberless idle words they speak. Therefore the Caliph ᶜUmar said, "Weigh

[14] Field has Amiya. This section in the Persian text, which adds numerous similar anecdotes on the authority of ᶜÂ'isha, Junayd, etc., is much abridged in the Field translation.

[15] The belief in two angels who record one's actions is derived from the Koran, 50:17-18: "Behold, two (guardian angels) appointed to learn (his doings), learn (and note them), One sitting on the right and one on the left" and 82:10-12, "Verily over you (are appointed angels) to protect you,—kind and honourable,—writing down (your deeds): They know (and understand) all that ye do."

[16] The Muslim "rosary" (*subḥah*) is a string of beads used by pious Muslims to keep count as they recite the ninety-nine beautiful names of God or other religious formulae such as the *takbîr* ("God is Great"), *tasbîḥ* ("O Holy God"), or *taḥmîd* ("God be praised"). The number of beads on the rosary varies, but it typically has one hundred: one for each of the "beautiful names" plus one for Allâh (God). It has been suggested that the Muslims copied the use of such prayer beads from the Buddhists, and the Crusaders later introduced the Muslim practice among Christians. See EI_1, 4:492.

well your words and deeds before they be weighed at the judgment." He himself, before retiring for the night, used to strike his feet with a scourge and exclaim, "What has thou done today?"

Abû Ṭalḥa[17] was once praying in a palm-grove, when the sight of a beautiful bird which flew out of it caused him to make a mistake in counting the number of prostrations he had made. To punish himself for his inattention, he gave the palm-grove away. Such saints knew that their sensual nature was prone to go astray, therefore they keep a strict watch over it, and punished it for each transgression.

If a man finds himself sluggish and averse from austerity and self-discipline he should consort with one who is proficient in such practices so as to catch the contagion of his enthusiasm. One saint used to say, "When I grow lukewarm in self-discipline, I look at Muḥammad b. Wâsiᶜ,[18] and the sight of him rekindles my fervor for at least a week." If one cannot find such a pattern of austerity close at hand, then it is a good thing to study the lives of the saints; he should also exhort his soul somewhat in the following way: "O my soul! thou thinkest thyself intelligent and art angry at being called a fool, and yet what else are thou, after all? Thou prepared clothing to shield thee from the cold of winter, yet makest no preparation for the after-life. Thy state is like that of a man who in mid-winter should say, 'I will wear no warm clothing, but trust to God's mercy to shield me from the cold.' He forgets that God, at the same time that He created cold, showed man the way to make clothing to protect himself from it, and provided the material

---

[17] Perhaps the Abû Ṭalḥa al-Mâlikî mentioned briefly by Hujwîrî/Nicholson, *Kashf al-maḥjûb*, p. 322.

[18] Famous as one of the "weepers" (*bukkâ'*) or ascetics who cry during their spiritual exercises. See Hujwîrî/Nicholson, *Kashf al-maḥjûb*, pp. 91-92; EI_2, 1:959.

for that clothing. Remember this also, O soul, that thy punishment hereafter will not be because God is angry with thy disobedience; and say not, 'How can my sin hurt God?' It is thy lusts themselves which will have kindled the flames of a hell within thee; just as, from eating unwholesome food, disease is caused in a man's body, and not because his doctor is vexed with him for disobeying his orders.

"Shame upon thee, O soul, for thy over-weening love of the world! If thou dost not believe in heaven or hell, at any rate thou believest in death, which will snatch from thee all worldly delights and cause thee to feel the pangs of separation from them, which will be intenser just in proportion as thou has attached thyself to them. Why art thou made after the world? If the whole of it, from East to West, were thine and worshiped thee, yet it would all, in a brief space, turn to dust along with thyself, and oblivion would blot out thy name, as those of ancient kings before thee. But now, seeing thou hast only a very small fragment of the world, and that a defiled one, wilt thou be so made as to barter eternal joy for it, a precious jewel for a broken cup of earthenware, and make thyself the laughing-stock of all around them?"

A Muslim Image of Paradise. This drawing depicts angels (or fairies) in a garden of delights; it reflects many of the popular notions about paradise that were based on a literal intrepretation of some Koranic verses. These may be contrasted with Ghazzâlî's views, which regard the beatific vision of God as the most sublime aspect of the hereafter. A sixteenth century Safavid drawing in the Freer Gallery of Art, accession #50.2. (Reproduced by permission of the Freer Gallery of Art, Smithsonian Institution, Washington D. C.)

Chapter Eight
The Love of God

[This is chapter nine of the "fourth cornerstone" in the Persian text. Ghazzâlî uses the mystic terminology *maḥabba*, *shawq*, and *riḍâ* to express the concept Field translates as "love of God."]

The love of God is the highest of all topics, and is the final aim to which we have been tending hitherto. We have spoken of spiritual dangers as they hinder the love of God in a man's heart, and we have spoken of various good qualities as being the necessary preliminaries to it. Human perfection resides in this, that the love of God should conquer a man's heart and possess it wholly, and even if it does not possess it wholly it should predominate in the heart over the love of all other things. Nevertheless, rightly to understand the love of God is so difficult a matter that one sect of theologians have altogether denied that man can love a Being who is not of his own species, and they have defined the love of God as consisting merely in obedience. Those who hold such views do not know what real religion is.

All Muslims are agreed that the love of God is a duty. God says concerning the believers, "He loves them and they love Him,"[1] and the prophet said, "Till a man loves God and His prophet more than anything else he has not the right faith." When the angel of death came to take the soul of Abraham the latter said, "Have you ever seen a friend take his friend's life?"

---

[1] The phrase in question comes from the Koran, 5:57; the terms "lovers" or "beloved" of God are often used to denote the Sufi mystics.

God answered him, "Have you ever seen a friend unwilling to see his friend?" Then Abraham said, "O ᶜAzrâ'îl![2] take my soul!" The following prayer was taught by the Prophet to his companions, "O God, grant me to love Thee and to love those who love Thee, and whatsoever brings me nearer to Thy love, and make Thy love more precious to me than cold water to the thirsty." Ḥasan Baṣrî[3] used to say, "He who knows God loves Him, and he who knows the world hates it."

We come now to treat of love in its essential nature. Love may be defined as an inclination to that which is pleasant. This is apparent in the case of the five senses, each of which may be said to love that which gives it delight; thus the eye loves beautiful forms, the ear music, etc. This is a kind of love we share with the animals. But there is a sixth sense, or faculty of perception, implanted in the heart, which animals do not possess, through which we become aware of spiritual beauty and excellence. Thus, a man who is only acquainted with sensuous delights cannot understand what the Prophet meant when he said he loved prayer more than perfumes or women, though the last two were also pleasant to him. But he whose inner eye is opened to behold the beauty and perfection of God will despise all outward sights in comparison, however fair they may be.

The former kind of man will say that beauty resides in red-and-white complexions, well proportioned limbs, and so forth,

---

[2] The name given in Islamic tradition for for the angel of death mentioned in Koran, 32:11.

[3] Abû Saᶜîd Ḥasan b. Abi'l-Ḥasan of Basra (21-110/542-728) was famous both for the rectitude of his life and the pious eloquence of his sermons and writings. The saying attributed to him here is typical of his proverbial remarks such as "Make this world into a bridge over which you cross but on which you do not build." See Arberry, *Saints and Mystics*, pp. 19-25; H. Ritter, "Studien zur Geschichte der islamischen Frömmigkeit, i.: Hasan el-Basri," *Der Islam* 21(1933):1-83.

but he will be blind to moral beauty, such as men refer to when they speak of such and such a man as possessing a "beautiful" character. But those possessed of inner perception find it quite possible to love the departed great, such as the Caliphs ᶜUmar and Abû Bakr, on account of their noble qualities, though their bodies have long been mingled with the dust. Such love is directed not towards any outward form, but towards the inner character. Even when we wish to excite love in a child towards anyone, we do not describe their outward beauty of form, etc., but their inner excellences.

When we apply this principle to the love of God we shall find that He alone is worthy of our love, and that, if anyone loves Him not, it is because he does not know Him. Whatever we love in anyone we love because it is a reflection of Him. It is for this reason that we love Muḥammad, because he is the Prophet and the Beloved of God, and the love of learned and pious men is really the love of God. We shall see this more clearly if we consider what are the causes which excite love.

The first cause is this, that man loves himself and the perfection of his own nature. This leads him directly to the love of God, for man's very existence and man's attribute are nothing else but the gift of God, but for whose grace and kindness man would never have emerged from behind the curtain of non-existence into the visible world. Man's preservation and eventual attainment to perfection are also entirely dependent upon the grace of God. It would indeed be a wonder, if one should take refuge from the heat of the sun under the shadow of a tree and not be grateful to the tree, without which there would be no shadow at all. Precisely in the same way, were it not for God, man would have no existence nor attributes at all; wherefore, then, should not he love God, unless he be ignorant of Him? Doubtless fools cannot love

Him, for the love of Him springs directly from the knowledge of Him, and whence should a fool have knowledge?

The second cause of this love is that man loves his benefactor, and in truth his only benefactor is God, for whatever kindness he receives from any fellow-creature is due to the immediate instigation of God. Whatever motive may have prompted the kindness he receives from another, whether the desire to gain religious merit or a good name, God is the Agent who set that motive to work.

The third cause is the love that is aroused by contemplation of the attributes of God, His power and wisdom, of which human power and wisdom are but the feeblest reflections. This love is akin to that we feel to the great and good men of the past, such as the Imâm Mâlik and the Imâm Shâfiᶜî,[4] though we never expect to receive any personal benefits from them, and is therefore a more disinterested kind of love. God said to the Prophet David, "That servant is dearest to Me who does not seek Me from fear of punishment or hope of reward, but to pay the debt due to My Deity." And in the Psalms[5] it is written, "Who is a greater transgressor than he who worships Me from fear of hell or hope of heaven? If I had created neither, should I not then have deserved to be worshiped?"

---

[4] Founders of two of the Sunni schools of law (*madhâhib*). Mâlik b. Anas (d. 179/795) was the author of a famous collection of traditions of the prophet, known as the *Muwaṭṭaᶜ*, who lived in Madina; Muḥammad b. Idrîs al-Shâfiᶜî (d. 204/820), author of some of the earliest and most authoritative treatises on Islamic legal theory and methodology, was born in Ghaza and spent most of his life in Baghdad and Egypt. The Persian text is somewhat different from the Field translation; it reads "such as Imâm Shâfiᶜî or other imâms of the Muslims."

[5] The *Zabûr*, a work attributed in the Koran to David; various ostensible copies of it, apparently Arabic translations from the Psalms and other works, were in circulation in early Islamic times. See EI_1, 4:1184-85.

The fourth cause of this love is the affinity between man and God, which is referred to in the saying of the Prophet, "Verily, God created man in His own likeness." Furthermore, God has said, "My servant seeks proximity to Me, that I may make him My friend, and when I have made him My friend I become his ear, his eye, his tongue."[6] Again, God said to Moses, "I was sick, and thou didst not visit Me?" Moses replied, "O God! Thou art Lord of heaven and earth: how couldest Thou be sick?" God said, "A certain servant of Mine was sick; hadst thou visited him, thou wouldst have visited Me."[7]

This is a somewhat dangerous topic to dwell upon, as it is beyond the understanding of common people, and even intelligent men have stumbled in treating of it, and come to believe in incarnation and union with God. Still, the affinity which does exist between man and God disposes of the objection of those theologians mentioned above, who maintain that man cannot love a being who is not of his own species. However great the distance between them, man can love God because of the affinity indicated in the saying, "God created man in His own likeness."

The Vision of God

All Muslims profess to believe that the Vision of God is the summit of human felicity, because it is so stated in the Law;[8]

---

[6] This is apparently a *ḥadîth qudsî*. It is very similar, though not identical, with a saying cited in Graham, *Divine Word*, p. 173.

[7] A fuller version of the famous *ḥadîth qudsî* quoted earlier by Ghazzali (see above, Chapter Two, n. 12); cf. Graham, *Divine Word*, p. 179.

[8] Cf. Ghazzâlî, *Mysteries*, pp. 71-73. The promise of actually seeing God in the hereafter is suggested by the Koran (54:55; 75:23) and maintained as a matter of dogma by many theologians: "We confess that the meeting of God with the inhabitants of Paradise will be a reality, without description,

but with many this is a mere lip-profession which arouses no emotion in their hearts. This is quite natural, for how can a man long for a thing of which he has no knowledge? We will endeavor to show briefly why the Vision of God is the greatest happiness to which a man can attain.

In the first place, every one of man's faculties has its appropriate function which it delights to fulfill. This holds good of them all, from the lowest bodily appetite to the highest form of intellectual apprehension. But even a comparatively low form of mental exertion affords greater pleasure than the satisfaction of bodily appetites. Thus, if a man happens to be absorbed in a game of chess, he will not come to his meal, though repeatedly summoned. And the higher the subject matter of our knowledge, the greater is our delight in it: for instance, we would take more pleasure in knowing the secrets of a king than the secrets of a vizier. Seeing, then, that God is the highest possible object of knowledge, the knowledge of Him must afford more delight than any other. He who knows God, even in this world, dwells, as it were, in a paradise, "the breadth of which is as the breadth of the heavens and the earth,"[9] a paradise the fruits of which no one can ever prevent him plucking, and the extent of which is not narrowed by the multitude of those who occupy it.[10]

---

comparison, or modality." (*Waṣîat Abî Ḥanîfa*, art. 24.) Although some sects, such as the Shi'ites, rejected the idea as anthropomorphic, the ecstatic vision of God was much celebrated by the mystics; the Persian poet Ḥâfiẓ, for example, writing, "This borrowed life which the Friend hath entrusted to Ḥâfiẓ—/One day I shall see His Face and yield it up to Him." (See E. G. Browne, *Literary History of Persia*, 3:301 n. 3).

[9] See the Koran, 57:21; 3:133. This is also the Koranic phrase which Ghazzâlî used to describe the condition of Muslim gnostics (*al-ʿârifûn*) in the *Jawâhir al-qur'ân;* see Abul Quasem, *The Jewels of the Qur'ân,* p. 17.

[10] Cf. Koran, 55:54; 56:20.

But the delight of knowledge still falls short of the delight of vision, just as our pleasure in thinking of those whose love is much less than the pleasure afforded by the actual sight of them. Our imprisonment in bodies of clay and water, and entanglement in the things of sense constitute a veil which hides the Vision of God from us, although it does not prevent our attaining to some knowledge of Him. For this reason God said to Moses on Mount Sinai, "Thou shalt not see Me."[11]

The truth of the matter is this, that, just as the seed of man becomes a man, and a buried datestone becomes a palm-tree, so the knowledge of God acquired on earth will in the next world change into the Vision of God, and he who has never learnt the knowledge will never have the Vision. This vision will not be shared alike by all who know, but their discernment of it will vary exactly as their knowledge. God is one, but He will be seen in many different ways, just as one object is reflected in different ways by different mirrors, some showing it straight, and some distorted, some clearly and some dimly. A mirror may be so crooked as to make even a beautiful form appear misshapen, and a man may carry into the next world a heart so dark and distorted that the sight which will be a source of peace and joy to others will be to him a source of misery. He, in whose heart the love of God has prevailed over all else, will derive more joy from this vision than he in whose heart it has not so prevailed; just as in the case of two men with equally powerful eyesight, gazing on a beautiful face, he who already loves the possessor of that face will rejoice in beholding it more than he who does not. For perfect happiness mere knowledge is not enough, unaccompanied by love, and the love of God cannot take possession of a man's heart till it be purified from love of the world, which purification can only be effected by

[11] Koran, 7:143.

abstinence and austerity. While he is in this world a man's condition with regard to the Vision of God is like that of a lover who should see his Beloved's face in the twilight, while his clothes are infested with hornets and scorpions, which continually torment him. But should the sun arise and reveal his Beloved's face in all its beauty, and the noxious vermin leave off molesting him, then the lover's joy will be like that of God's servant, who, released from the twilight and the tormenting trials of this world, beholds Him without a veil. Abû Sulaymân[12] said, "He who is busy with himself now will be busy with himself then, and he who is occupied with God now will be occupied with Him then."

Yaḥyâ b. Muᶜâdh[13] relates, "I watched Bâyazîd Bisṭâmî[14] at prayer through one entire night. When he had finished he stood up and said, 'O Lord! some of Thy servants have asked and obtained of Thee the power to perform miracles, to walk on the sea, and to fly in the air, but this I do not ask; some have asked and obtained treasures, but these I do not ask.' Then he turned, and, seeing me, said, 'Are you there, Yaḥyâ?' I replied, 'Yes.' He asked, 'Since when?' I answered, 'For a long time.' I then asked him to reveal to me some of his spiritual

---

[12] al-Dârânî; see above, Chapter Five, n. 6.

[13] Yaḥyâ b. Muᶜâdh al-Râzî, one of the Sufis of Nishapur; d. 258/871. See Arberry, *Saints and Mystics*, pp. 179-82; Schimmel, *Mystical Dimensions*, pp. 51-52.

[14] The reference is to Bâyazîd (abbreviated form of Abû Yazîd) al-Bisṭâmî (d. between 261/874 and 264/878), one of the most famous of the early Muslim mystics, who lived in seclusion near the town of Bisṭâm in eastern Iran. None of his writings (if he produced any) have survived; there was an order of mystics which claimed to be based on his teachings. Like Ghazzâlî, he probably combined asceticism and mysticism with absolute respect for the religious law. See Arberry, *Saints and Mystics*, pp. 100-123; EI_2, 1:162-63; A. J. Arberry, "A Bisṭâmî Legend," *Journal of the Royal Asiatic Society* (1938), pp. 89-91; Schimmel, *Mystical Dimensions*, pp. 47-51.

experiences. 'I will reveal,' he answered, 'what is lawful to tell you. The Almighty showed me His kingdom, from its loftiest to its lowest; He raised me above the throne and the seat and all the seven heavens. Then He said, "Ask of me whatsoever thing thou desirest." I answered, "Lord! I wish for nothing beside Thee." "Verily," He said, "thou art My servant."'"

On another occasion Bâyazîd said, "Were God to offer thee the intimacy with Himself or Abraham, the power in prayer of Moses, the spirituality of Jesus, yet keep thy face directed to Him only, for He has treasures surpassing even these." One day a friend said to him, "For thirty years I have fasted by day and prayed by night and have found none of that spiritual joy of which thou speakest." Bâyazîd answered, "If you fasted and prayed for three hundred years, you would never find it." "How is that?" asked the other. "Because," said Bâyazîd, "your selfishness is acting as a veil between you and God." "Tell me, then, the cure." "It is a cure which you cannot carry out." However, as his friend pressed him to reveal it, Bâyazîd said, "Go to the nearest barber and have your beard shaved; strip yourself of your clothes, with the exception of a girdle round your loins. Take a horse's nose-bag full of walnuts, hang it around your neck, go into the bazaar and cry out, 'Any body who gives me a slap on the nape of my neck shall have a walnut.' Then, in this manner, go where the Qadi and the doctors of the law are sitting." "Bless my soul!" said his friend, "I really can't do that, do suggest some other remedy." "This is the indispensable preliminary to a cure," answered Bâyazîd, "but, as I told you, you are incurable."

The reason Bâyazîd indicated this method of cure for want of relish in devotion was that his friend was an ambitious seeker after place and honor. Ambition and pride are diseases which can only be cured in some such way. God said unto Jesus, "O Jesus! when I see in My servants' hearts pure love for

Myself unmixed with any selfish desire concerning this world or the next, I act as guardian over that love." Again, when people asked Jesus, "What is the highest work of all?" he answered, "To love God and to be resigned to His will." The saint Râbiᶜa[15] was once asked whether she loved the Prophet: "The love of the Creator," she said, "has prevented my loving the creature." Ibrâhîm b. Adham,[16] in his prayers, said, "O God! in my eyes heaven itself is less than a gnat in comparison with the love of Thee and the joy of Thy remembrance which thou hast granted me."

He who supposes that it is possible to enjoy happiness in the next world apart from the love of God is far gone in error, for the very essence of the future life is to arrive at God as at an object of desire long aimed at and attained through countless obstacles. The enjoyment of God is happiness. But if he had no delight in God before, he will not delight in Him then, and if his joy in God was but slight before it will be but slight then. In brief, our future happiness will be in strict proportion to the degree in which we have loved God here.

---

[15] Rabîᶜa al-ᶜAdawiyya (ca. 95/713-185/801) was probably the most famous female mystic in Islam. She lived in celibacy and asceticism at Basra, attracting many disciples who became famous in their own right. Much of her poetry has been preserved; it emphasizes a doctrine of disinterested love of God for His own sake, nor out of fear of punishment or hope of reward. See Arberry, *Saints and Mystics*, pp. 39-51; Margaret Smith, *Râbiᶜa the Mystic and her Fellow-saints in Islam* (Cambridge, 1928).

[16] Another famous Muslim mystic, Ibrâhîm b. Adham was in later legend a prince of the city of Balkh in eastern Iran who heard a voice rebuke him while hunting and so "abandoned the path of worldly pomp for the path of asceticism and piety." Many scholars have noted the possible influence of Buddhism on this story. He reportedly died while participating in a naval expedition against the Byzantine empire (between 160/776 and 166/783). See Arberry, *Saints and Mystics*, pp. 62-79; R. A. Nicholson, "Ibrâhim b. Adham," *Zeitschrift für Assyriologie* 26(1912):215-20; EI_2, 3:985-86.

But (and may God preserve us from such a doom!) if in a man's heart there has been growing up a love of what is opposed to God, the conditions of the next life will be altogether alien to him, and that which will cause joy to others will to him cause misery.

This may be illustrated by the following anecdote: A certain scavenger went into the perfume-sellers' bazaar, and, smelling the sweet scents, fell down unconscious. People came round him and sprinkled rose-water upon him and held musk to his nose, but he only became worse. At last one came who had been a scavenger himself; he held a little filth under the man's nose and he revived instantly, exclaiming, with a sigh of satisfaction, "Ah! this is perfume indeed!" Thus in the next life a worldling will no longer find the filthy lucre and the filthy joys of the world; the spiritual joys of that world will be altogether alien to him and but increase his wretchedness. For the next world is a world of Spirit and of the manifestation of the Beauty of God; happy is that man who has aimed at and acquired affinity with it. All austerities, devotions, studies have the acquirement of that affinity for their aim, and that affinity is love. This is the meaning of that saying of the Koran, "He who has purified [his soul] is happy." Sins and lusts directly oppose the attainment of this affinity; therefore the Koran goes on to say, "and he who has corrupted [his soul] is miserable."[17] Those who are gifted with spiritual insight have really grasped this truth as a fact of experience, and not a merely traditional maxim. Their clear perception of it leads them to the conviction that he by whom it was spoken was a prophet indeed, just as a man who has studied medicine knows when he is listening to a physician. This is a kind of certainty which requires no support from miracles such as the

[17] Koran, 91:9-10; the phrases in brackets have been interpolated by the translator.

conversion of a rod into a snake, the credit of which may be shaken by apparently equally extraordinary miracles performed by magicians.

The Signs of the Love of God

Many claim to love God, but each should examine himself as to the genuineness of the love which he professes. The first test is this: he should not dislike the thought of death, for no friend shrinks from going to see a friend. The Prophet said, "Whoever wishes to see God, God wishes to see him." It is true a sincere lover of God may shrink from the thought of death coming before he has finished his preparation for the next world but if he is sincere, he will be diligent in making such preparation.

The second test of sincerity is that a man should be willing to sacrifice his will to God's. He should cleave to what brings him nearer to God, and should shun what places him at a distance from God. The fact of a man's sinning is no proof that he does not love God at all, but it proves that he does not love Him with his whole heart. The saint Fuḍayl[18] said to a certain man, "If anyone asks you whether you love God, keep silent; for if you say, 'I do not love Him,' then you are an infidel; and if you say, 'I do,' your deeds contradict you."

The third test is that the remembrance of God should always remain fresh in a man's heart without effort, for what a man loves he constantly remembers, and if his love is perfect he never forgets it. It is possible, however, that, while the love of God does not take the first place in a man's heart, the love

---

[18] Abû ᶜAlî Fuḍayl b. ᶜIyâd al-Ṭâliqânî (d. 187/803). Originally a highway robber, he converted to Sufism and became a great exponent of asceticsm. See Arberry, *Saints and Mystics*, pp. 52-61; EI_2, 2:936.

of the love of God may, for love is one thing and the love of love another.

The fourth test is that he will love the Koran, which is the Word of God, and Muḥammad, who is the Prophet of God; if his love is really strong, he will love all men, for all are God's servants, nay, his love will embrace the whole creation, for he who loves anyone loves the works he composes and his handwriting.

The fifth test is, he will be covetous of retirement and privacy for purposes of devotion, he will long for the approach of night, so that he may hold intercourse with his Friend [i.e., God] without let or hindrance. If he prefers conversation by day and sleep at night to such retirement, then his love is imperfect. God said to David, "Be not too intimate with men; for two kinds of persons are excluded from My presence: those who are earnest in seeking reward and slack when they obtain it, and those who prefer their own thoughts to the remembrance of Me. The sign of My displeasure is that I leave such to themselves."

In truth, if the love of God really takes possession of the heart all other love is excluded. One of the children of Israel was in the habit of praying at night, but, observing that a bird sang in a certain tree very sweetly, he began to pray under that tree, in order to have the pleasure of listening to the bird. God told David to go and say to him, "Thou hast mingled the love of a melodious bird with the love of Me; thy rank among the saints is lowered." On the other hand, some have loved God with such intensity that, while they were engaged in devotion, their houses have caught fire and they have not noticed it.

A sixth test is that worship becomes easy. A certain saint said, "During one space of thirty years I performed my night-devotions with great difficulty, but during a second space of thirty years they became a delight." When love of God is complete no joy is equal to the joy of worship.

The seventh test is that lovers of God will love those who obey Him and hate the infidels and the disobedient, as the Koran says: "They are strenuous against the unbelievers and merciful to each other."[19] The Prophet once asked God and said, "O Lord, who are Thy lovers?" and the answer came, "Those who cleave to Me as a child to its mother, take refuge in the remembrance of Me as a bird seeks the shelter of its nest, and are as angry at the sight of sin as an angry lion who fears nothing."

[Several pages at the end of this chapter in the Persian text are omitted in the Field translation. It is followed by a chapter on death which concludes both the fourth "cornerstone" and the book as a whole.]

---

[19] Koran, 48:29.

A Ghazzâlî Bibliography

WORKS BY AL-GHAZZÂLÎ

*al-Arba*ᶜ*în fî uṣûl al-dîn*. Edited Cairo, 1344/1925.

[Theological treatise using commentary on selected verses from the Koran; a continuation of the *Jawâhir al-qur'ân*. Brief excerpt in J. Robson. "Al-Ghazâlî and the Sunna." *Muslim World* 45(1955):324-333.]

Ayyuhâ al-walad. Facsimile of Arabic manuscript in George Scherer. *O Youth!* Beirut, 1933.

[A short ethical treatise; the original was written in Persian. Translations: Facsimile of Arabic manuscript with English translation by George Scherer. *O Youth!* Beirut, 1933. German translation by Joseph von Hammer-Purgstall. *O Kind!* Vienna, 1838. French translations by Toufic Sabbagh. *Lettre au disciple*. Beirut, 1959. Renon, A. "L'Éducation des enfants dès le premier âge, par l'Imâm al-Ghazâlî, texte et traduction." *Institut des belles lettres arabes* 8(1945):57-74. Excerpts in M. Ben Cheneb. "Lettre sur l'éducation des enfants." *Revue africaine* 45(1901):101-110. Spanish translation by Esteban Lator. *Oh hijo!* Beirut, 1951.]

al-Basîṭ.

[Still in manuscript. A short treatise on problems of jurisprudence, perhaps based on lecture notes, presented to Ghazzâlî's teacher, Juvaynî; it is certainly one of Ghazzâlî's earliest writings.]

Bayân faḍâ'iḥ al-ibâḥiyya.

[A condemnation of antinomianism in Islam. Edited and translated by Otto Pretzl. *Die Streitschrift des Gazâlî gegen die Ibâhîja*. Munich, 1933.]

Bidâyat al-hidâya. Edited by M. al-Ḥalabî. Cairo, 1344/1912.

[A theory of the foundations of outward piety. Translations: M. Abul Quasem. *Al-Ghazâlî on Islamic Guidance*. Selangor, 1979. Also in W. M. Watt. *The Faith and Practice of al-Ghazâlî*. London, 1953. Pp. 86-152. J. Heil. *Die Religion des Islam*. Jena, 1915.]

al-Durra al-fâkhira. Edition by L. Gautier. *Ad-dourra al-fâkhira*. Leipzig, 1877 and Geneva, 1878.

[An eschatological work on Judgment Day and the hereafter; the attribution to Ghazzâlî has been questioned, though it is generally assumed that he wrote it late in life. Translations: Jane Smith. *The Precious Pearl*. Missoula, Mont., 1979. German translation by Mohamed Bergsch. *Die Kostbau Perle im Wissen des Janseits*. Hanover, 1924. French translation by Lucien Gautier. *Ad-dourra al-fâkhira, la perle précieuse de Ghazâlî*. Geneva, 1878.]

Faḍâ'iḥ al-bâṭiniyya wa faḍâ'il al-mustaẓhiriyya. Edited by ᶜAbd al-Raḥman Badawî. Cairo, 1964.

[Ghazzâlî's critique of Fatimid Shiʿism and defense of the Abbasid caliphate in general and the rule of the Caliph al-Mustaẓhir in particular; also known simply as the *Mustaẓhirî*. Translations: In R. McCarthy. *Freedom and Fulfillment*. Boston, 1980. Pp. 175-286. Abridged translation by Ignaz Goldziher. *Streitschrift des Gazâlî gegen die Bâtinijja-Sekte*. Leiden, 1916.]

Faḍâ'il al-anâm. Edited by ᶜAbbâs ᶜIqbâl. Tehran, 1333/1954.

[A collection of letters written in Persian by Ghazzâlî to various prominent personalities in which he frequently disavows the political life. Translations: Dorothea Krawulsky. *Briefe und Reden des Abû Hâmid Muhammad al-Gazzâlî, übersetzt und erläeutert von Dorothea Krawulsky*. Freiburg, 1971. Abdul Qayyum. *Letters of al-Ghazzali*. Lahore, 1976. French and Arabic translations in Nûr al-Dîn Âl Ali. *Letters of al-Ghazzâlî on Islamic Topics*. Tunis, 1972.]

Fâtiḥat al-ᶜulûm. Cairo, 1322/1904.

[Similar to Book I of the *Ihyâ'*.]

al-Fayṣal al-tafriqa bayn al-islâm wa'l-zandaqa. Edited S. Dunyâ. Cairo, 1381/1961.

[Primarily a critique, written at least partly in self-defense, of the intolerance and divisiveness of theology and a liberal plea not to brand any believer a heretic without good reason. Translations: In R. McCarthy. *Freedom and Fulfillment*. Boston, 1980. Pp. 145-174. Edition and French translation by Hogga Mustapha. *Le critère décisif de distinction entre l'Islam et le Manicheisme*. Casablanca, 1983. See also H. Runge. *Über Gazâlî's Faiṣal al-tafriqa*. Kiel 1938.]

al-Ḥikma fî makhlûqât allâh. Edited by M. al-Qubbânî al-Dimashqî. Cairo, 1321/1903.

[A treatise on how creation reveals the wisdom of God at work.]

Iḥyâ' ᶜulûm al-dîn. Edited Bulâq, 1289/1872-73; Cairo, 1327/1910; etc.

[Ghazzâlî's greatest work; a comprehensive guide to worship, everyday life, and mystical experience. Synopsis: G. H Bousquet. *Ih'ya ᶜouloûm ed-dîn; ou, Vivification des sciences de la foi. Analyse et index par G.-H. Bousquet, avec la collaboration d'un groupe d'arabisantes et d'arabisants*. Paris, 1955.

Partial Translations:

Book I: Nabih Faris. *The Book of Knowledge*. Lahore, 1966.

Book II: Nabih Faris. *The Foundations of the Articles of the Faith*. Lahore, 1963. Hans Bauer. *Die Dogmatik al-Ghazâlî's nach dem II. Buche seines Hauptwerkes*. Halle, 1912.

Book IV: Edwin Calverley. *Worship in Islam*. London, 1925.

Book V: Nabih Faris. *The Mysteries of Almsgiving*. Beirut, 1966. Excerpts in Muhtar Holland. *Al-Ghazzali on the Duties of Brotherhood*. London, 1975.

Book VIII: Muhammad Abul Quasem. *The Recitation and Interpretation of the Qur'an*. London, 1979.

Book IX: Translated by Najiro Nakamura. *Ghazzali on Prayer*. Tokyo, 1973.

Book XI: H. Kindermann. *Über die guten Sitten beim Essen und Trinken.* Leiden, 1964.

Book XII: Madelain Farah. *Marriage and Sexuality in Islam.* Salt Lake City, 1984. French translation by G. Bousquet and L. Bercher. *Le Livre des bon usages en matière de mariage.* Paris, 1935. German translation by Hans Bauer. *Von der Ehe.* Halle, 1917.

Book XIV: Hans Bauer. *Erlaubtes und verbotenes Gud.* Halle, 1922.

Book XVIII: D. B. Macdonald. "Emotional Religion in Islam as Affected by Music and Singing." *Journal of the Royal Asiatic Society* (1901), pp. 195-252, 705-748; (1902), pp. 1-28.

Book XIX: Léon Bercher. *L'Obligation d'ordonner le bien et d'interdire le mal.* Tunis, 1961.

Book XX: Leon Zolondek. *Book XX of al-Ghazâlî's "Iḥyâ' ᶜulûm ad-Dîn".* Leiden, 1963.

Book XXI: In R. McCarthy. *Freedom and Fulfillment.* Boston, 1980. Pp. 363-82. Karl Eckmann. *Die Wunder des Herzens.* Excerpt in L. Gardet. "Texte d'Al-Ghazâlî traduit et annoté." *Revue thomiste* 44(1938):569-78.

Book XXIII: Excerpts in L. Bercher. "Extrait du livre XXIII du *Kitâb iḥya 'ulûm ad-dîn* d'Al-Gazali (chapitre de la concupiscence charnelle)." *Hesperides* 40(1953):313-331.

Book XXXI: Susanna Wilzer. "Untersuchungen zu Gazzâlî's *Kitâb at-tauba.*" *Der Islam* 32:237-309, 33:51-120, 34:128-37

Book XXXIII: William McKane. *Al-Ghazali's Book of Fear and Hope.* Leiden, 1962.

Book XXXV: Hans Wehr. *al-Gazzâlî's Buch von Gottvertrauen.* Halle, 1940.

Books XXXI-XXXVI: Richard Gramlich. *Muhammad al-Ghazzâlîs Lehre von den Stufen zür Gottesliebe.* Wiesbaden, 1984.

Book XXXVII: Hans Bauer. *Über Intention.* Halle, 1916.

Book XXXVIII: Excerpt in L. Gardet. "L'Abandon à Dieu (tawakkul), presentation et traduction d'un texte d'Al-Ghazzâlî." *Institut des belles lettres arabes* 13(1950):37-48.

Book XL: T. J. Winter. *The Remembrance of Death and the Afterlife*. Cambridge, 1989.]

Iljâm al-ᶜawâmm ᶜan ᶜilm al-kalâm. Edited Cairo, 1351/1932.

[Perhaps Ghazzâlî's last work; a theological refutation of anthropomorphism, but with a warning not to expose common people to the dangers of theology.]

al-Imlâ' ᶜalâ ishkâlât al-iḥyâ'. In *Mulḥaq iḥyâ' ᶜulûm al-dîn*. Beirut, n. d.

[A response to criticism of his *Iḥyâ'* and his personal justification for writing it; probably composed just before Ghazzâlî's death.]

al-Iqtiṣâd fi'l-iᶜtiqâd. Edited Ankara, 1962.

[An evaluation of what rational theology can and cannot contribute to a religious life. Translations: Excerpts in ᶜAbd al-Rahman Abu Zayd. *Al-Ghazzali on Divine Predicates and Their Properties*. Lahore, 1970. Spanish translation by Miguel Asín Palacios. *El justo medio en la creencia*. Madrid, 1929.]

Jawâhir al-qur'ân. Cairo, 1911.

[Theological treatise with Commentary on selected verses from the Koran. Translated by M. Abul Quasem. *The Jewels of the Qur'ân* London, 1983.]

al-Kashf wa'l-tabyîn fî ghurûr al-khalq ajmaᶜîn. Cairo, 1279/1862-63.

[On disobedience to God.]

Khulâṣat al-taṣânîf fi'l-taṣawwuf. Cairo, n. d.

[A treatise on Sufism; translated from Persian into Arabic. It is apparently an Arabic recension of the Persian original of *Ayyuhâ al-walad*.]

Kîmîâ-yi sa^c^âdat. Edited by Ḥusayn Khadîv-jam. Tehran, 1361/1983.

[Translations: H. A. Homes. *The Alchemy of Happiness by M. al-Ghazzali the Mohammedan Philosopher*. Albany, 1873. Claud Field. *The Alchemy of Happiness*. London, 1910. Hellmut Ritter. *Das Elixir der Glückseligkeit*. Jena, 1923.]

Kîmîâ' al-sa^c^âda. Edited by Muḥammad ^c^-bd al-^c^Alîm. Cairo, n. d.

[An Arabic recension of the chapter on "Knowledge of Self" from the *Alchemy*.]

al-Maḍnûn bihi ^c^alâ ghayr ahlihi. Printed in the margin of ^c^Abd al-Karîm al-Jîlî. *al-Insân al-kâmil*. Cairo, 1949.

[A treatise on eschatology, angels, miracles; similar to the Iljâm in arguing that such theological material should not be disclosed to ordinary believers. Translations: Abdul Qayyum Shafaq Hazarvi. *The Mysteries of the Human Soul*. Lahore, 1981. Excerpts in M. Asín Palacios. *La Espiritualidad de Algazel y su sentido cristiano*. Madrid, 1934-41. Pp. 609-91.]

al-Maḍnûn al-ṣaghîr.

[Translations: Excerpts in M. Asín Palacios. *La Espiritualidad de Algazel y su sentido cristiano*. Madrid, 1934-41. Pp. 692-733.]

al-Mankhûl fî uṣûl al-fiqh.

[Still in manuscript. A commentary on legal problems, probably based on notes taken from Juvaynî's lectures.]

Maqâṣid al-falâsifa. Edited Cairo, 1331/1912.

[A summary of Ghazzâlî's investigations into the teachings of the philosophers. See Georg Beer. *Al-Gazzali's Maḳâṣid al-falâsifat*. Leiden, 1888. Translations: Miguel Alonso Alonso. *Maqâsid al-falâsifa: o intenciones de los filósofos*. Barcelona, 1963. The Latin translation (Venice, 1506) is edited in J. T. Muckle. *Algazel's Metaphysics*. Toronto, 1933.]

al-Maqṣad al-asnâ' fî sharḥ ma^cânî asmâ' allâh al-ḥusnâ. Edited by F. Shehadi. Beirut, 1971.

[Also known as *al-Maqṣad al-aqṣâ*. A treatise on the ninety-nine beautiful names of God found in the Koran and often chanted during Sufi dhikrs. Translations: In R. McCarthy. *Freedom and Fulfillment*. Boston, 1980. Pp. 333-362. Robert Stade. *Ninety-nine Names of God in Islam*. Ibadan, 1970]

Miḥakk al-naẓar fi'l-manṭiq. Edited by M. al-Na[c]sânî and M. al-Qubbânî. Cairo, 1925.

[A textbook on logic; one of Ghazzâlî's early works.]

Minhâj al-[c]âbidîn. In *al-Quṣûr al-[c]awâlî*. Cairo, 1964.

[Reportedly dictated at the very end of Ghazzâlî's life. Translations: Ernst Bannerth. *Der Pfad der Gottesdiener*. Salzburg, 1964.]

Mishkât al-anwâr. Edited by [c]Abd al-[c]Alâ [c]Afîf. Cairo, 1964.

[A commentary on Chapter XXXV of the Koran, the "Chapter of Light," developing the concept of the "inner light" of mysticism leading to the greater "Light" of God; regarded as one of Ghazzâlî's last works. Translations: W. H. T. Gairdner. *Al-Ghazzâlî's Mishkât al-anwâr ("The Niche for Lights")*. London, 1924.]

Mi[c]yar al-[c]ilm fî fann al-manṭiq. Edited by M. S. Kurdî. Cairo, 1329/1911.

[A treatise on logic.]

Mîzân al-[c]amal. Edited by M. S. Kurdî and M. Nu[c]aymî. Cairo, 1328/1910

[A treatise on practical ethics in the light of religious knowledge. Translations: Hikmat Hachem. *Critère de l'action (Mîzân al-a[c]mal); traité d'ethique psychologique et mystique*. Paris, 1945.]

Mukâshafat al-qulûb. Abridged edition Bulâq, 1300/1882-83.

[A treatise on ethics.]

al-Munqidh min al-ḍalâl. Edited by A. Maḥmûd. Cairo, 1952.

[Translations: In R. McCarthy. *Freedom and Fulfillment*. Boston, 1980. Pp. 61-114. W. M. Watt. *The Faith and Practice of al-Ghazâlî*. London, 1953. Pp. 19-85. Claud Field. *The Confessions of al-Ghazzali*. London, 1909. French translation by Farid Jabre. *Al-Munqid min adalal: Erreur et délivrance*. Beirut, 1959. Dutch translation by J. H. Kramers. *De redder uit de dwaling*. Amsterdam, 1951. M. C. Barbier de Meynard. "Traduction nouvelle du traité de Ghazzali intitulé le Préservatif de l'erreur. *Journal Asiatique* n. s. 9(1887):5-93.]

al-Mustaṣfâ min ᶜilm al-uṣûl. Bulâq, 1325/1907; reprint Baghdad, 1970.

[One of Ghazzâlî's early works; a treatise on the sources of law.]

Naṣîḥat al-mulûk. Edited by Jalâl al-Dîn Humâ'î. Tehran, 1361/1983.

[A book in Persian on the nature and ethics of kingship. Translation: F. R. C. Bagley. *Ghazâlî's Book of Counsel for Kings*. London, 1964.]

Qawâṣim al-bâṭiniyya.

[A polemic against the Bâtinîs. Text and Turkish translation by Ahmet Ateş. Istanbul University, *Ilâhiyat Fakültesi Dergisi* 3(1954):23-54.]

al-Qisṭâs al-mustaqîm. Edited Cairo, 1303/1885-86. Also edited by Père V. Chelhot. Beirut, 1959.

[Translations: In R. McCarthy. *Freedom and Fulfillment*. Boston, 1980. Pp. 287-332. V. Chelhot in *Bulletin des Études Orientales* 15:7-98.]

al-Radd al-jamîl ᶜalâ sarîḥ al-injîl. Edited by R. Chidiac. Paris, 1939.

[A polemical treatise against Christianity. Translations: F. Wilms. *al-Ghazâlîs Schrift wider die Gottheid Jesu*. Leiden, 1966. R. Chidiac. *Réfutation excellente de la divinité de Jésus Christ d'après les Evangiles*. Paris, 1939.]

al-Risâla al-laduniyya. Cairo, 1910.

[On the intuition which allows Sufis to receive knowledge directly from God. Translations: Margaret Smith. "Al-Risâlat al-laduniyya." *Journal of the Royal Asiatic Society* (1938):177-200, 353-374. Excerpt in L. Gardet. "Qu'est-ce que l'homme?" *Institut des belles lettres arabes* 7(1944):395-426.]

al-Risâla al-qudsiyya. Arabic text in Tibawi (cited below).

[Also known as the *Qawâ*ᶜ*id al-*ᶜ*aqâ'id*. An epistle on Islamic doctrine addressed to the people of Jerusalem in 489/1096; more or less identical to Book II of the *Iḥyâ'*. Translation: A. Tibawi. "Al-Ghazâlî's Tract on Dogmatic Theology." *Islamic Quarterly* 9(1965):65-122.]

Risâlat al-ṭayr. Edited Cairo, 1353/1934-35.

[An argument for salvation by faith, thought to be aimed at Ibn Sînâ. Translation: Nabih Faris. "Ghazzali's Epistle of the Birds. A Translation of the Risâlat al-ṭayr." *Muslim World* 34(1944):46-53.

*Risâla fi'l-wa*ᶜ*ẓ wa'l-i*ᶜ*tiqâd*. Cairo, 1325/1907.

[A letter to Abu'l-Fatḥ of Mosul, expressing anti-Muᶜtazilî ideas similar to those of Book III of the *Iḥyâ'* and the *Iljâm al-*ᶜ*awâmm*.]

Shifâ' al-ghalîl. Edited by Ḥamad Kubaysî. Baghdad, 1971.

[A treatise on law and *uṣûl al-fiqh* dedicated to Juvaynî.]

Tahâfut al-falâsifa. Edited by Maurice Bouyges. Beirut, 1927.

[One of Ghazzâlî's most famous works, written ca. 487/1094, containing his systematic critique of the shortcomings and errors of rational philosophy. Translations: S. A. Kamali. *Al-Ghazali's Tahafut al-falasifa: Incoherence of the Philosophers*. Lahore, 1963. Excerpts in M. Asín Palacios. *La Espiritualidad de Algazel y su sentido cristiano.* Madrid, 1934-1941. Pp. 745-880. Partial translation by B. Carra de Vaux. In *Le Muséon* 18(1900):143-57, 274-308, 400-408; n. s. 1(1901):346-77.]

al-Taḥbîr fî ᶜilm al-taᶜbîr.

[Still in manuscript. A work, dubiously attributed to Ghazzâlî, dealing with the interpretation of dreams.]

al-Tibr al-masbûk. Cairo, 1968.

[Arabic translation of the Persian *Naṣîḥat al-mulûk.*]

al-Wajîz. Cairo, 1317/1899-1900.

[A short treatise on Shâfiᶜî jurisprudence.]

al-Waṣîṭ.

[Still in manuscript. A revised version of *al-Baṣîṭ*, an earlier treatise on jurisprudence.]

WORKS ABOUT AL-GHAZZÂLÎ

Abd el-Jalil, J. M. "Autour de la sincérité d'al-Ghazzali." In *Mélanges Louis Massignon* 1(1956):57-72.

Abu Hamid al-Ghazzali: Proceedings of the International Conference Held in Commemoration of the 9th Centenary of His Birth. Cairo, 1967.

Abu Rida, M. *al-Ghazâlî und seine Widerlegung der griechischen Philosophie.* Madrid, 1952.

Abu Shanah, R. E. "The Philosophical Significance of al-Ghazzâlî." *Iqbal Review* 13(1972):51-70.

Abul Quasem, M. "Al-Ghazâlî's Conception of Happiness." *Arabica* 22(1975):153-61.

——. "Al-Ghazâlî's Rejection of Philosophic Ethics." *Islamic Studies* 12(1974):111-27.

——. "Al-Ghazâlî's Theory of Devotional Acts." *Islamic Quarterly* 18(1972):48-61.

——. "Al-Ghazâlî's Theory of Good Character." *Islamic Culture* (1978):229-39.

——. *The Ethics of al-Ghazzâlî.* Petaling Jaya, Selangor, 1975.

Aguilar, E. G. "Sur un livre récent: La notion de la Ma'rifa chez Ghazzali par Farid Jabre." *Institut des belles lettres arabes* 21(1958):213-20.

Ali, S. N. *Some Religious and Moral Teachings of al-Ghazzali.* Baroda, 1921.

Alonso, M. A. "Influencia de Algazel en el mundo latino." *Al-Andalus* 23(1958):371-80.

Antes, Peter. *Prophetenwunder in der As^câriyya bis al-Gazâlî (Algazel).* Freiburg, 1970.

Arkoun, M. "Révélation, vérité et histoire d'après l'oeuvre des Gazâlî." *Studia Islamica* 31(1970):53-69.

Arnaldez, Roger. *Controverses theologiques chez Ibn Hazm de Cordoue et Ghazali.* Paris, 1956.

Asín Palacios, Miguel. *Algazel, Dogmatica, Moral y Ascetica.* Zaragoza, 1901.

———. *La Espiritualidad de Algazel y su sentido cristiano.* Madrid, 1934-41.

———. *La Mystique d'al-Ghazâlî.* Beirut, 1914.

———. "El Origen del lenguaje y problemas conexos en Algazel, Ibn Sina, e Ibn Ḥazm." *Al-Andalus* 4(1936):253-81.

———. *Los Precedentes musulmanes del 'Pari' de Pascal.* Santander, 1920.

———. "Sens du mot Teháfot dans les oeuvres d'El-Ghazâli et d'Averroès." *Revue africaine* 50(1906):185-203.

Auerbach, Heimann. *Albalag und seine Übersetzung des Maqasid al-Gazzalis.* Breslau, 1906.

Badâwî, [c]Abd al-Raḥmân. *Mu'allafât al-Ghazzâlî.* Cairo, 1961.

Barny, F. J. "The Moslem Idea of *'ilm* (Knowledge) illustrated by Al Ghazali's Experience." *Muslim World* 9(1919):159-68.

Bauer, Hans. "Zum Titel und zur Abfassung von Ghazâlî's Iḥjâ." *Der Islam* 4(1913):159-60.

Beaurecueil, S. "Gazzâlî et S. Thomas d'Aquin." *Bulletin de l'Institut français d'archéologie orientale (Caire)* 46(1947):199-238.

Beer, Georg. *Al-Gazzali's Maḳâṣid al-falâsifat*. Leiden, 1888.

Bello, Iysa. *The Medieval Islamic Controversy Between Philosophy and Orthodoxy: Ijmâ^c and Ta'wîl in the Conflict between al-Ghazâlî and Ibn Rushd*. Leiden, 1989.

Bercher, L. "La Censure des moeurs selon Ghazzali." *Institut des belles lettres arabes* 18(1955):313-21; 20(1957):21-30; 21(1958):389-407; 23(1960):299-326.

Binder, Leonard. "al-Ghazali's Theory of Islamic Government." *Muslim World* 45(1955):229-41.

Blasdell, R. "Religious Values in al-Ghazâlî's Works." *Muslim World* 36(1946):115-20.

Boer, T de. *Die Widersprüche der Philosophie nach al-Gazzâlî*. Strassburg, 1894.

Borrmans, M. "Note sur l'observation de la nature et son utilisation chez Abû Hamid Muhammad al-Ghazâlî." *Institut des belles lettres arabes* 21(1958):117-52.

Bouyges, Maurice. *Essai de chronologie des oeuvres de al-Ghazali*. Beirut, 1959. [Revised by Michel Allard.]

Cabanelas, D. "Un Capítulo inédito de Algazel sobre la 'razón'." *Miscelánea de estudios árabes y hebraicos* 8(1958):29-46.

——. "Notas para la historia de Algazel en España." *Al-Andalus* 17(1952):223-32.

——. "Un Opúsculo inédito de Algazel: el 'Libro de las intuiciones intelectuales'." *Al-Andalus* 21(1956):19-58.

Calverley, E. E. "The Dialogue between Al Ghazâlî and the Philosophers on the Origin of the World." *Muslim World* 48(1958):183-91.

Carra de Vaux, Baron Bernard. *Les grands philosophes. Gazali*. Paris, 1902.

Chelhot, V. "Al-Qisṭâs al-Mustaqîm et la connaissance rationelle chez Gazâlî." *Bulletin des Études Orientales* 15(1955-57):7-98.

Chertoff, G. B. *The Logical Part of al-Ghazzâlî's Maqâsid al-falâsifa*. Ph. D. thesis; Columbia, 1952.

Çubukçu, Ibrahim. *Gazzalî ve batinîlik*. Ankara, 1964.

———. *Gazzalî ve süphecilik*. Ankara, 1964.

Davids, T. "Does Al Ghazzali Use an Indian Metaphor?" *Journal of the Royal Asiatic Society* (1911):200-201.

Demeerseman, A. "Ce qu'Ibn Khaldoun pense d'Al-Ghazzâlî." *Institut des belles lettres arabes* 21(1958):161-93.

———. "Le Maghreb a-t-il une marque ghazzâlienne?" *Institut des belles lettres arabes* 21(1958):109-16.

Dingemans, Herman. *al-Ghazâlî's boek der liefde*. Leiden, 1938.

Donaldson, Dwight. "The Ethical Teachings of al-Ghazálí." In *Studies In Muslim Ethics*. London, 1953. Pp. 134-65.

———. "Mohammed al-Ghazzali." *Muslim World* 11(1921):377-88.

———. "A Visit to the Grave of Al Ghazzali." *Muslim World* 8(1918):137-40.

El-Taher Uraibi, M. *Al-Ghazalis aporien im Zusammenhang mit dem Kausalproblem*. Bonn, 1972.

Ettinghausen, R. "Al-Ghazzâli on Beauty." *Art and Thought* (1947):160-65.

Faris, Nabih. "al-Ghazzali's Rules of Conduct." *Muslim World* 32(1942):43-54.

———. "The Iḥyâ' 'Ulûm al-Dîn of al-Ghazzâlî." *Proceedings of the American Philosophical Society* 71(1939):15-19.

Foster, F. "Ghazali on the Inner Secret and Outward Expression in his 'Child'." *Muslim World* 23(1933):378-96.

Frick, H. *Ghazâlî's Selbstbiographie: ein Vergleich mit Augustins Konfessionem*. Leipzig, 1919.

Gairdner, W. H. T. "Al-Ghazâlî's Mishkât al-Anwâr and the Ghazâlî Problem." *Der Islam* 5(1914):121-53.

Gardener, W. R. W. "al-Ghazali as Sufi." *Muslim World* 7(1917):131-43.

——. *An Account of al-Ghazâlî's Life and Works*. Madras, 1919.

Gätje, H. "Logisch-semasiologische Theorien bei al-Gazzâlî." *Arabica* 21(1974):151-88.

Goodman, Lenn. "Ghazâlî's Argument from Creation." *International Journal of Middle East Studies* 2(1971):67-85, 168-88.

——. "Did al-Ghazâlî Deny Causality?" *Studia Islamica* 47(1978):83-120.

Gosche, Reinhard. *Über Ghazâlî's Leben und Werke*. Berlin, 1858.

Gottheil, R. "A Supposed Work of al-Ghazâlî." *Journal of the American Oriental Society* 43(1923):85-91.

Hitzig, F. "Ueber Gazzâlî's *Iḥja ᶜulûm al-dîn*." *Zeitschrift der Deutschen Morgenländischen Gesellschaft* 7(1853):172-86.

Holland, Muhtar. *Inner Dimensions of Islamic Worship.* Leicester, 1983. [Excerpts from the *Iḥyâ'*.]

Hourani, George. "The Chronology of Ghazâlî's Writings." *Journal of the American Oriental Society* 79(1959):225-33.

——. "The Dialogue Between al-Ghazâlî and the Philosophers on the Origin of the World." *Muslim World* 48(1958):308-14.

Jabre, Farid. "La Biographie et l'oeuvre de Ghazâlî reconsidérées à la lumière des Ṭabaqât de Sobkî." *Mélanges de l'Institut Dominicain d'Études Orientales du Caire* 1(1954):73-102.

——. *Essai sur le lexique de Ghazali: contribution à l'étude de la terminologie de Ghazali*. Beirut, 1970.

____. "L'Extase de Plotin et le Fanâ' de Ghazâlî." *Studia Islamica* 6(1956):101-24.

——. *La Notion de certitude selon Ghazzali dans ses origines psychologiques et historiques*. Paris, 1958.

——. *La Notion de la maᶜrifa chez Ghazali*. Beirut, 1958.

Kamali, S. A. *Types of Islamic Thought in Criticism and Reconstruction.* Aligarh, 1963. [Comparison of Ghazzâlî's *Tahâfut* and Ibn Taymiyya's *Radd.*]

Karam, J. "La requisitoria de Algazel contra los filósofos." *Ciencia tomista* 61(1941):234-314.

Karim, Maulana Fazul-ul. *Imam Gazzali's Ihya Ulum id-din.* Lahore, n. d.

Kempfner, G. "Rationalisme et mystique: à propos d'Al-Ghazzali." *Institut des belles lettres arabes* 21(1958):153-60.

Kerimov, G. M. *Al-Gazali i Sufizm.* Baku, 1969.

Khan, Shafique. *Ghazali's Philosophy of Education.* Hyderabad, 1976.

Krachkovskii, I. "Rukopis Destructio philosophorum al-Gazâlî v Aziatskom Muzee." *Doklady Rossiiskoi Akademii Nauk.* Ser. B(1925):47-49.

Lambton, A. K. S. "The Theory of Kingship in the *Naṣîhat ul-Mulûk* of Ghazâlî." *Islamic Quarterly* 1(1954):47-55.

Laoust, Henri. *La Politique de Gazâlî.* Paris, 1970.

———. "La Survie de Gazâlî d'après Subkî." *Bulletin des Études Orientales* 25(1972):153-72.

Lazarus-Yafeh, H. *Étude sur la polémique islamo-chrétien.* Paris, 1969. [On the authenticity of the *Radd al-jamîl.*]

———. "Philosophical Terms as a Criterion of Authenticity in the Writings of Al-Ghazzâlî." *Studia Islamica* 25(1966):111-21.

———. "The Place of the Religious Commandments in the Philosophy of al-Ghazâlî." *Muslim World* 51(1961):173-84.

———. *Studies in al-Ghazzali.* Jerusalem, 1975.

Lelong, M. "Actualité de Ghazzali." *Institut des belles lettres arabes* 21(1958):195-212.

LeTourneau, R. "Al-Ghazâlî et Ibn Toûmert se sont-ils recontrés?" *Bulletin des études arabes* 7(1947):147-48.

Lohr, C. H. "Logica Algazeli: Introduction and Critical Text." *Traditio* 21(1965):223-290.

Macdonald, Duncan B. "The Life of al-Ghazzâlî." *Journal of the American Oriental Society*, 20(1899):71-132.

——. "Meanings of the Philosophers by al-Ghazzâlî." *Isis* 25(1936):9-15.

Malter, H. *Die abhandlung des Abu Hâmid al-Gazzâli*. Frankfurt, 1896.

Ma^c^lûf, Louis. *Onze traités philosophiques*. Beirut, 1908.

Marmura, M. E. "Ghazali and Demonstrative Science." *Journal of the History of Philosophy* 3(1965):183-204.

——. "The Logical Role of the Argument from Time in the Tahâfut's Second Proof for the World's Pre-Eternity." *Muslim World* 49(1959):306-14.

Marzouki, Abu Yaarub. *Le Concept de causalité chez Gazali*. Tunis, 1978.

Massignon, L. "Le Christ dans les évangiles, selon Ghazâlî." *Revue des études islamiques* 6(1932):523-36.

Michot, Jean. "Avicenne et le Kitâb al-Madnûn d'al-Ghazâlî." *Bulletin de Philosophie Medievale* (1975), pp. 52-59.

Moulder, D. C. "The First Crisis in the Life of Alghazâlî." *Islamic Studies* 11(1972):113-23.

Naish, C. G. "Al Ghazali on Penitence." *Muslim World* 16(1926):6-18.

Najm, S. M. "The Place and Function of Doubt in the Philosophies of Descartes and al-Ghazâlî." *Philosophy East and West* 16(1966):133-41.

Naumkin, V. V. *Voskreshenie nauk o vere*. Moscow, 1980. [Russian translation of parts of the *Iḥyâ'*.]

Nawab Ali, Syed. *Some Moral and Religious Teachings of al-Ghazzali*. Lahore, 1944.

Obermann, J. *Der philosophischen und religiöse Subjektivismus Gazâlîs*. Vienna, 1921.

Ormsby, Eric. *An Islamic Version of Theodicy: the dispute over al-Ghazîlî's "best of all possible worlds."* Ph.D. Thesis; Princeton, 1981.

———. *Theodicy in Islamic Thought*. Princeton, 1984.

Othman, Ali. *The Concept of Man in Islam in the Writings of al-Ghazali*. Cairo, 1960.

Padwick, Constance. "al-Ghazali and the Arabic Version of the Gospels: An Unsolved Problem." *Muslim World* 29(1939):130-40.

Pedersen, J. "Ein Gedicht al-Gazâlî's." *Monde Oriental* 25(1931):230-349.

Pennings, G. J. "God's Decrees and Man's Responsibility. An Attempt by al-Ghazali to Reconcile the Two." *Muslim World* 31(1941):23-28.

Poggi, Vincenzo. *Un classico della spiritualità musulmana: Saggio monografico sul "Munqid" di al-Gazâlî*. Rome, 1967.

Politella, J. "al-Ghazzali and Meister Eckhart: Two Giants of the Spirit." *Muslim World* 54(1964):100-194; 233-44.

ur-Rahim, Reza. "Al-Ghazâlî's Shifâ' al-Ghalîl." *Islamic Studies* 2(1963):399-401.

Rahman, S. M. "Al-Ghazzali." *Islamic Culture* 1(1927):406-11.

Ritter, H. *Aphorism über die Leibe*. Istanbul, 1942.

Rolston, Holmes. *Religious Inquiry: Participation and Detachment*. New York, 1985. [A comparative study of Augustin, Ghazzâlî, and Nagarjuna.]

Runge, Hans. *Über Gazâlî's Faisal al-tafriqa baina-l-islâm wa'l-zandaqa*. Kiel, 1938.

Schmoelders, Augustus. *Essai sur les écoles philosophiques chez les Arabes, et notamment sur la doctrine d'Algazzali*. Paris, 1842.

Shafaq, S. R. "Some Abiding Teachings of al-Ghazâlî." *Muslim World* 44(1954):43-48.

Shah, Idries. *Four Sufi Classics*. London, 1980. [Includes a translation from the *Mishkât al-anwâr*.]

Shehadi, Fadlou. *Ghazali's Unique Unknowable God*. Leiden, 1964.

Sheikh, M. "al-Ghazali's Influence on the West." *Pakistan Philosophical Journal* 11(1973):53-67.

Sherif, Mohammed. *Ghazali's Theory of Virtue*. Albany, 1975.

Sherwani, H. "El-Ghazzali on the Theory and Practice of Politics." *Islamic Culture* 9(1935):450-74.

Siauve, M. L. *L'Amour de Dieu chez Gazali: une philosophie de l'amour à Bagdad au début du XIIe siècle*. Paris, 1986.

Smith, Margaret. "The Forerunner of al-Ghazali." *Journal of the Royal Asiatic Society* (1936):65-78.

——. "al-Ghazâlî on the Practice of the Presence of God." *Muslim World* 23(1933):16-27.

——. *Al-Ghazâlî the Mystic*. London, 1944.

Steiner, Heinrich. *Die Mu^c taziliten als Vorläufer der islâmschen Dogmatiker und Philosophen. Nebst Anhang, enthaltend kritische Anmerkungen zu Gazzâlî's Munkid*. Leipzig, 1865.

Stern, Martin. *Al-Ghazzâlî on Repentance*. Ph.D. Thesis; UCLA, 1977.

Tomeh, G. J. "The Climax of a Philosophical Conflict in Islam." *Muslim World* 42(1952):172-89.

Ülken, Hilmi. "Les Traductions en turc de certains livres d'al-Ghazali." *Ilâhiyat Fakültesi Dergisi* 9(1961):70-79.

Umaruddin, M. *The Ethical Philosophy of al-Ghazzâlî*. Aligarh, 1962.

Upper, C. R. "Al-Ghazâlî's Thought Concerning the Nature of Man and Union with God." *Muslim World* 42(1952):23-32.

Vaglieri, Laura and Rubinacci, Roberto. *Scritti scelti di al-Ghazâlî*. Turin, 1970.

Vajda, Georges. *Isaac Albalag: averroiste juif, traducteur et annotateur d'al-Ghazâlî*. Paris, 1960.

Van Den Bergh, S. "Ghazali on 'Gratitude towards God' and its Greek Sources." *Studia Islamica* 7(1957):77-98.

——. "The 'Love of God' in Ghazali's *Vivification of Theology*." *Journal of Semitic Studies* 1(1956):305-21.

Van Leeuvwen, Arend. "Essai de bibliographie d'al-Ghazzâlî." *Institut des belles lettres arabes* 21(1958):221-27.

——. *Ghazâlî als apologeet van der Islam*. Leiden, 1947.

Watt, W. M. "A Forgery in al-Ghazâlî's Mishkât?" *Journal of the Royal Asiatic Society* (1949):5-22.

——. "The Authenticity of the Works Attributed to al-Ghazzâlî." *Journal of the Royal Asiatic Society* (1952):24-45.

——. *Muslim Intellectual*. Edinburgh, 1963.

——. "Reflections on Al-Ghazâlî's Political Theory." *Glascow Oriental Society Transactions* 21(1965-66):12-24.

——. "The Study of al-Gazâlî." *Oriens* 13-14(1960-61):121-31.

Wensinck, A. J. "Ghazalî's Mishkât al-anwâr." *Semietische Studien*. Leiden, 1941.

——. "Un Juicio de conjunto sobre Algazel." *Al-Andalus* 11(1946):485-88.

——. *La Pensée de Ghazzâlî*. Paris, 1940.

——. *On the Relation between al-Ghazâlî's Cosmology and His Mysticism*. Amsterdam, 1933.

Wickens, G. M. "The 'Persian Letters' Attributed to al-Ghazâlî." *Islamic Quarterly* 3(1956):109-16.

Wolfson, H. "Avicenna, Algazali, and Averroes on Divine Attributes." *Homenaje a Millás Vallicrosa* 2(1956):545-71.

——. "Nicolaus of Autrecourt and Ghazâlî's Argument Against Causality." *Speculum* 44(1969):234-38.

Wolfson, J. *Der Einfluss Gazali's auf Chisdai Crescas.* Frankfurt, 1905.

Zedler, Beatrice Hope. *Destructio destructionum philosophiae Algazelis in the Latin version of Calo Calonymos*. Milwaukee, 1961.

Zuberi, Masarrat Husein. *Aristotle, 384-322 B.C. and al-Ghazali, 1058-1111 A.D.* Karachi, 1986.

Zwemer, S. M. "James Rendel Harris on al-Ghazali." *Muslim World* 32(1942):51-54.

——. *A Moslem Seeker After God; Showing Islam at Its Best in the Life and Teaching of al-Ghazali*. New York, 1920.

——. *The Place Given to Christ in Ghazali's Ihya*. Cairo, 1917.

Elton L. Daniel is Associate Professor of History and Director of the World Civilization Program at the University of Hawaii. He is the author of *The Social and Political History of Khurasan under Abbasid Rule* and *A Shi'ite Pilgrimage to Mecca* as well as numerous articles on early Islamic and Iranian history.